Language Proficiency and Academic Achievement

Multilingual Matters

1. "Bilingualism: Basic Principles"
   HUGO BAETENS BEARDSMORE

2. "Evaluating Bilingual Education: A Canadian Case Study"
   MERRILL SWAIN AND SHARON LAPKIN

3. "Bilingual Children: Guidance for the Family"
   GEORGE SAUNDERS

4. "Language Attitudes Among Arabic-French Bilinguals in Morocco"
   ABDELÂLI BENTAHILA

5. "Conflict and Language Planning in Quebec"
   RICHARD Y. BOURHIS (ed.)

6. "Bilingualism and Special Education"
   JIM CUMMINS

7. "Bilingualism or Not: The Education of Minorities"
   TOVE SKUTNABB-KANGAS

8. "An Ethnographic/Sociolinguistic Approach to Language Proficiency Assessment"
   CHARLENE RIVERA (ed.)

9. "Communicative Competence Approaches to Language Proficiency Assessment: Research and Application"
   CHARLENE RIVERA (ed.)

10. "Language Proficiency and Academic Achievement"
    CHARLENE RIVERA (ed.)

11. "Pluralism: Cultural Maintenance and Evolution"
    BRIAN BULLIVANT

12. "Placement Procedures in Bilingual Education: Education and Policy Issues"
    CHARLENE RIVERA (ed.)

13. "The Education of Linguistic and Cultural Minorities in the OECD Countries"
    STACY CHURCHILL

MULTILINGUAL MATTERS 10

Language Proficiency and Academic Achievement

Edited by
Charlene Rivera

MULTILINGUAL
MATTERS LTD

Multilingual Matters Ltd
Bank House, 8a Hill Road
Clevedon, Avon BS21 7HH
England

Copyright © 1984 InterAmerica Research Associates
All Rights Reserved. No part of this work
may be reproduced in any form or by any
means without permission in writing from
the publisher

Copyright is claimed until seven years
from date of publication. Thereafter
all portions of the work covered by
this copyright will be in the public
domain.

The work was developed under a
contract with the United States
Department of Education. However
the content does not necessarily
reflect the position or policy
of that agency and no official
endorsement of these materials
should be inferred.

British Library Cataloguing in Publication Data

Language proficiency and academic achievement.
 – (Multilingual matters; 10)
 1. Bilingualism   2. Academic achievement
 I. Rivera, Charlene
 401   LB1131

ISBN 0-905028-24-4
ISBN 0-905028-23-6 Pbk

Production co-ordination and jacket design by
MM Productions Ltd, 1 Brookside, Hertford, Herts SG13 7LJ

Typeset by Herts Typesetting Services, Hertford.
Printed and bound in Great Britain by Robert Hartnoll Ltd., Bodmin, Cornwall.

To Dick, mom and dad for their loving support.

Contents

ACKNOWLEDGEMENTS	viii
PREFACE	ix
BACKGROUND TO THE LANGUAGE PROFICIENCY ASSESSMENT SYMPOSIUM	xv
	xix

Wanted: A Theoretical Framework for Relating Language Proficiency to Academic Achievement Among Bilingual Students
    Jim Cummins 2

On Cummins' Theoretical Framework
    Fred Genessee 20

On Some Theoretical Frameworks for Language Proficiency
    Michael Canale 28

A Note on the Dangers of Terminological Innovation
    Bernard Spolsky 41

SCALP: Social and Cultural Aspects of Language Proficiency
    Rudolph C. Troike 44

A Sociolinguistic Perspective on Cummins' Current Framework for Relating Language Proficiency to Academic Achievement
    Benji Wald 55

Language Proficiency and Academic Achievement Revisited: A Response
    Jim Cummins 71

INDEX 77

Acknowledgements

This volume would not have been possible without the support of the National Institute of Education and InterAmerica Research Associates. It would not have become a reality without the assistance of many dedicated individuals. It is with much gratitude that they are here recognized.

Reynaldo Macias, the former NIE Assistant Director for Reading and Language Studies and Ellen Rosansky, the first NIE ALPBP Project officer supported the concept of the LPA Symposium and encouraged the formalization of this volume Dan Ulibarri, who later became the NIE ALPBP Project Officer, also provided invaluable encouragement in its finalization. Carmen Simich-Dudgeon, the ALPBP Research Associate, assisted in the initial conceptualization of the LPA Symposium and through her in depth understanding of the issues which concern bilingual educators and her knowledge of sociolinguistics and ethnography contributed greatly to the volume. Mary Cunningham, the LPA Symposium coordinator, who skillfully handled all of the Symposium logistics, helped to locate interested publishers for the volume. The fruits of her efforts are here realized. Eileen Shaw, the technical editor, spent unending hours reviewing and editing manuscripts. She together with Elizabeth Gannon, who verified all references, provided moral support and encouragement throughout the preparation of this volume.

Finally, I would like to thank the National Academy of Education who through a Spencer Foundation Grant have made it possible for me to dedicate time and resources in the final production of this book.

Charlene Rivera
former ALPBP Project Director
Visiting Scholar
NAEP Project
Educational Testing Service

Preface

The great population shifts occurring throughout the world today have focussed attention on language policy in the education of children who do not speak the language of the country in which they are being schooled. The establishment of guest-worker policies in Europe and Australia and politically-motivated migrations of peoples from regions such as Southeast Asia and the Caribbean are some of the events that have brought about this situation. As Kloss observes,

> "Until recently, it was possible to venture an admittedly crude generalization regarding the global issue of language maintenance vs. language shift. Africa and the Americas, so the statement went, were leaning toward language shift in order to reduce the number of tribal tongues, and in the New World, also of immigrant tongues. In Europe and Asia, on the other hand, the psychological climate was held to be more favorable to language retention. This juxtaposition is beginning to get blurred, chiefly because so many American nations are moving toward greater freedom for maintenance — as a concomitant — for the unfolding of nondominant languages." (1977, p. iii)

Although the official language of the Federal government has always been English, historically the United States has not been a strictly monolingual country in either the speech of its people or its governments. State and local polities with high concentrations of people speaking other languages, at various times, have conducted their affairs in languages other than English: Spanish in Puerto Rico, French in some parishes of Louisiana and counties of Maine, German in Pennsylvania and Ohio, and Spanish in the Southwest and New York City.

Current Census data indicate that over 65 languages are spoken by a large number of citizens; recognition of the distinction among the Native

This volume was prepared as part of the Assessment of Bilingual Persons Project supported in part through the National Institute of Education's contract (N.I.E. 400-79-002) with InterAmerica Research Associates. The Opinions of the contributors are their own and do not reflect those of the National Institute of Education.

American languages would add even more. The linguistic diversity brought on by earlier waves of immigration continues today as new waves of Vietnamese, Cambodians and Iranians enter this country (Kloss, 1977). The cost and consequences of the different approaches being used in the United States to educate such children are, therefore, of great interest not only within this country, but also to those concerned with the social, economic and political fabric of many other countries.

Schools have used diverse instructional methods for children from families speaking languages other than English. Some have taught in English in a sink or swim fashion or with the variant of adapting the English used to the students' comprehension. Some combine special tutoring in English, English as a Second Language (ESL), with use of English as the language of the classroom. If the student seems more proficient in the native language than in English, in addition to ESL instruction, some schools provide academic instruction in the student's first language. Still others, particularly in the early grades, provide almost all formal instruction in the students' first language, phasing in ESL while the child becomes literate in the native language.

Decisions about instructional approaches are influenced by considerations other than that of the learner's mastery of English. For example, some major factors considered include the number of language minority students, language diversity, availability of qualified teachers, costs, and attitudes toward language acquisition and maintenance. In making a decision about instructional approaches various theories concerning the nature of language proficiency essential for success in school along with an understanding of the impact of the various instructional approaches on the development of language skills and overall student achievement are important components. Often at the core of such a discussion are beliefs about the what and the how of language proficiency assessment.

The purposes of the Assessment of the Language Proficiency of Bilingual Persons (ALPBP) project were, first, to bring together what is known about these issues and, second, to improve understanding of language proficiency assessment in ways that would be practical for classroom teachers. The result, it was hoped, would be to provide constructs for thinking about language proficiency that could lead to practical tools for teachers' use and to better informed entry/exit decisions.

Points of Origin

There were several points of origin for the ALPBP project. One was the

1978 Falmouth Conference on Testing, Teaching and Learning (Tyler & White, 1979). This conference came about as a result of the 1978 conference called by the Department of Health, Education and Welfare (DHEW) which focused on the reasons for the decline in achievement test scores. Participants at the DHEW conference argued that a significant factor in the decline was the use of inappropriate tests. Using this line of reasoning the Falmouth Conference participants concluded that testing could serve important purposes if it was done in a different manner. They recognized that the use of standardized testing was often inefficient and unreliable, particularly, when used to make educational decisions about individuals and about program effectiveness. This was found to be particularly true in light of findings from human cognition studies. Thus, the participants urged Federal support of new approaches to testing:

> "How are we to pursue this vision of testing merged into a teaching-testing system, fitted to the natural classroom situation, drawing upon the cognitive scientists and teachers and scholars in the subject areas, and exploiting the rapidly developing information-handling technology? One way is to continue and perhaps expand support for research on classroom process and human cognition, and for the development of new technologically-based testing, and testing involving persons from the subject area." (Tyler & White, 1979, p. 12)

Another point of origin was a national survey of language minority students (O'Malley, 1981) and a project to develop entry-exit criteria for bilingual education programs (Southwest, 1980). Despite the usefulness of the results of these projects, their development was marked by some concern for the inadequacy of language proficiency assessment measures. The researchers used the best of what was known in order to carry out the survey and to develop criteria recognized that the time had arrived to put resources into the kind of studies that could contribute to the overall improvement of language proficiency assessment procedures, a view supported by many researchers (e.g. Cazden et al., 1972; Cummins, 1979; Carrasco et al., 1978; Hymes, 1976).

A third point of origin was the enthusiasm shown by many involved in language proficiency assessment for what variously had been called interactive research, collaborative development and developmental research. The notion is that knowledge and application have for too long been separated. More effective research, it has been recognized, can be carried out if researchers and practitioners work together as co-equal members of a team. A few models of such interactive research have been carried out (e.g. Tikunoff *et al.*, 1979; Tikunoff *et al.*, 1980; Philips, 1980; Shalaway & Lanier, 1979) and their results seem promising.

Other points of origin were the thinking that went into research agenda-building for the 1978 Congressionally mandated bilingual education studies, the funding of the Center for Research on Bilingualism, and the bilingual research concerns of the National Institute of Education's Teaching and Learning Program. The scores of papers, workshops, analyses, conferences and meetings leading into these activities laid some of the foundations for the project.

The issues which emerged from these activities and experiences precipitated NIE to develop an RFP which called for interactive research and which focused on issues related to language proficiency assessment. The RFP states that,

"Two of the most pressing needs in educating children from minority language backgrounds are (1) to pursue fundamental research on the nature of language proficiency and how it can be measured, and (2) to provide teachers with up-to-date knowledge of language proficiency assessment so they can improve their classroom assessment practices. The purpose of the RFP is to solicit proposals for a program of work with two parts: (1) the administration of a competitive research program to support fundamental research on language proficiency assessment and (2) the operation of an experimental program of teacher training designed to introduce teachers to current research perspectives on language proficiency assessment." (NIE, 1979, p. 5)

Arrivals

How successful has the effort been?

First, educational decisions are not likely to be better than our understanding of language acquisition, language functioning and the nature of language and its uses. While the finest crucible for promoting understanding may be theory-based, hypothesis-testing strong inference studies, another way of assessing depth of understanding is to determine if it can be applied. In this sense, the project has been successful.

Second, one of the functions of research is to help illuminate the way issues are thought about. It should improve ability to speak in more precise terms, and to refine the debates that go on as people seek their way toward new policies. Although a consensus on what is known about the nature of language proficiency and how it can be measured may not have been reached, the ALPBP project effort should at least clarify points of disagreement, reasons for them, and frame the issues even more constructively. Here also the results were commensurate with the considerable effort invested in the ALPBP project.

Third, the effort to form a working definition of communicative competence and language proficiency and to make practical recommendations which would be useful to teachers in the assessment of language minority students for the purpose of making better entry/exit decisions and for the improvement of classroom practice: Here our reach exceeded our grasp and the fundamental research. Although many definitions and descriptions are offered in the papers in this volume, it was not possible to reach a consensus with regard to a working definition of communicative competence.

Determining how many children in this country are language minority, deciding which of their needs are uniquely language related, and what services may meet those needs are tasks which are likely to engage attention for some time to come. Definitions and their applications may influence estimates of resources needed, distribution of resources, and the nature of programs, as well as the fate of individual students. Hoping for clean-cut guidance on any of these issues is ambitious. They are, however, all important and the ALPBP project seems to have brought together the most that good research, carefully and creatively pursued, can offer at this time.

Lois-ellin Datta
former Associate Director
NIE Program in Teaching
and Learning

Notes
1. Opinions are the author's and do not represent the position of the National Institute of Education.

References

Carrasco, R. L., Vera, A., & Cazden, C. V. 1978, Aspects of bilingual students' communicative competence in the classroom: A case study. Paper presented at the National Conference on Chicano and Latino Discourse Behavior, Princeton, N.J., April.
Cazden, C., John, V., & Hymes, D. (eds) 1972, *Functions of language in the classroom*. New York: Teachers College Press.
Cummins, J. 1979, Linguistic interdependence and the educational development of bilingual children. *Review of Educational Research*, 49(2), 222–51.

Hymes, D. 1976, Ethnographic measurement. Paper presented at the Symposium on Language Development in a Bilingual Setting, Pamona, CA, March.

Kloss, H. 1977, *The American bilingual tradition*. Rowley, Mass.: Newbury House Publishers.

National Institute of Education, 1979, Assessing the language proficiency of bilingual persons (RFP No. NIE-R-79-0012). Washington, D.C., Author, May.

O'Malley, J. M. 1981, *Children's English and services study: Language minority children with limited English proficiency in the United States*. Washington, D.C.: InterAmerica Research Associates, Inc., and the National Clearinghouse for Bilingual Education.

Philips, D. 1980, What do the researcher and the practitioner have to offer each other? *Educational Researcher*, 9(11), 17–20; 24.

Shalaway, L. & Lanier, J. 1979, Teachers collaborate in research. *New England Teacher Corps Exchange*, 2(3), 1–2.

Southwest Regional Laboratory for Educational Research and Development. 1980, *Resources for developing a student placement system for bilingual programs*. Washington, D.C.: U.S. Department of Health, Education and Welfare.

Tikunoff, W. J., Ward, B. A. & Griffin, G. A. 1979, *Interactive research and development on teaching* (Final report). San Francisco, CA: Far West Regional Laboratory.

Tikunoff, W. J., Ward, B. A. & Lazar, C. 1980, Partners: Teachers, researchers, trainer/developers – An interactive approach to teacher education R & D. In D. E. Hall, S. M. Hord & B. Brown (eds), *Exploring issues in teacher education: Questions for future research*. Austin, TX: The Research and Development Center for Teacher Education.

Tyler, R. W. & White, S. J. 1979, *Testing, teaching and learning*. Washington, D.C.: U.S. Department of Health, Education and Welfare.

Background to the language proficiency assessment symposium

This and the accompanying three volumes are composed of selected papers which were presented at the Language Proficiency Assessment Symposium (LPA), held March 14–18, 1981, at the Airlie House Conference Center in Warrenton, Virginia. The Symposium was planned and implemented as a component of the Assessment of Language Proficiency of Bilingual Persons (ALPBP) project. The goals of the ALPBP project, funded by the National Institute of Education (NIE, 1979) and administered by InterAmerica Research Associates, Inc., were:

— to pursue fundamental research on the nature of language proficiency and how it can be measured; and
— to provide teachers with up-to-date knowledge of language proficiency assessment (issues) so they can improve their classroom assessment practices (p. 5).

The LPA Symposium represented a major effort toward integrating both the insights gained from findings emerging from the research component and the implementation of the teacher training programs of the ALPBP project. The Symposium provided a forum where a broad spectrum of researchers, practitioners, and policymakers met to discuss the major issues and research findings which affect language proficiency assessment practices.

Researchers were represented by scholars involved in the development of models of communicative competence, related empirical research, and the development and validation of tests of language proficiency and/or communicative competence. Practitioners included teachers and school administrators engaged in the implementation of programs which require the application of language proficiency assessment strategies. Policymakers were individuals who play an important role in the funding of education research projects related to language proficiency assessment and who are influential in the establishment of policy in this area.

The participants interacted through the presentation of papers, reactions to presentations, and informal discussions. The main goals of the Symposium were selected by the organizers based on the issues identified in a survey of researchers and educators.

The goals were:

— to develop a working definition of communicative proficiency;
— to make recommendations for the assessment of language minority students for the purpose of entry/exit into appropriate educational programs; and
— to make recommendations for further research and to develop a research agenda.

In regard to the first goal, the Symposium participants acknowledged the need to clarify the nature and scope of communicative competence and its relationship to language proficiency. It was evident that some agreement among researchers and practitioners, along with much more conclusive information about the nature of language and how it should be measured, would be necessary to clarify the concepts. However, the recognized knowledge gaps and the diversity of perspectives, theories and research findings concerning the nature of language and its measurement, prevented the LPA Symposium participants from reaching a consensus. Issues which related to this topic are found in the volume, *Communicative Competence Approaches to Language Proficiency Assessment: Research and Application.* The issues discussed range from theoretical questions regarding the construct of communicative proficiency to research relating communicative proficiency to literacy related skills. Language tests and testing methodologies are considered in several papers. Questions are raised as to what tests should be measuring and why. The reliability of currently-used language proficiency assessment instruments, as well as the development of new, more appropriate measures are also addressed.

Issues related to the second goal are found in this and the subsequent three volumes. *An Ethnographic Sociolinguistic Approach to Language Proficiency Assessment* takes a multidisciplinary approach to language proficiency assessment and supports the development of innovative methods for analyzing patterns of children's language use. The research presented involves what has been called ethnographic/sociolinguistic approaches which places emphasis on the understanding of language use through the observation of children's language in naturally-occurring contexts. These approaches are in contrast to the use of traditional testing and experimental research methodologies.

The relationship between a learner's first and second language development and performance in school are the focus of this volume *Language Proficiency and Academic Achievement*. "A major reason for the confused state of the art of language proficiency in bilingual programs ... stems from the failure to develop an adequate theoretical framework for relating language proficiency to academic achievement," argues Cummins. He contends that without such a "framework it is impossible either to develop rational entry/exit criteria for bilingual programs or to design testing procedures to assess these criteria". The validity of the framework proposed by Cummins is debated in this volume.

The concerns of practitioners, researchers and policymakers, which relate to the assessment and placement of language minority students in bilingual education programs, are the theme of the volume *Placement Procedures in Bilingual Education: Educational and Policy Issues*. This volume focuses on the legal and practical implications of federal guidelines with regard to language proficiency assessment practices.

In meeting the third goal, the LPA Symposium provided a structure for participants to make practical recommendations directed at influencing federal and state policies regarding language proficiency assessment research and practices. The papers in all four volumes represent the participants' understanding of the various issues. The following is a summary of the conclusions reached and the recommendations made by the three groups represented at the Symposium — researchers, practitioners and policymakers.

The primary concerns of the researchers were:

— The need for basic research into the nature of language that can provide the foundation for clarifying the concept of communicative competence and its relationship to language proficiency;
— The need for applied research that expands on current understanding of the state of the art of language proficiency assessment;
— The need to undertake validation studies of currently available language proficiency assessment instruments;
— The development of multiple language assessment strategies that include both quantitative and qualitative components;
— The need for adaptable government guidelines that affect language proficiency assessment practices;
— The need for yearly meetings between researchers and practitioners to exchange information and ideas.

The major issues identified by the practitioners were:
— The need for a working definition of communicative competence that clarifies its relationship to language proficiency;
— The establishment of practical as well as adaptable federal guidelines affecting language proficiency assessment practices;
— The importance of maintaining a network of communication between practitioners and researchers;
— The importance of obtaining up-to-date information on language proficiency assessment practices through more extensive use of resources such as the National Clearinghouse for Bilingual Education (NCBE);
— The use of the LPA Symposium as a model for future meetings among practitioners, researchers and policymakers involved in language proficiency assessment practices that affect minority language students;
— The support of federal agencies in encouraging collaborative research, an example of which would be including as criteria in Requests for Proposals (RFPs) the participation of practitioners at the local level.

The issues of most importance, as seen by the policymakers, were:
— The need to establish federal guidelines that can be adapted to accommodate relevant research findings that have bearing on the application of language proficiency assessment practices;
— The need for federal agencies such as NIE and OBEMLA to continue to support applied research on issues related to language proficiency assessment through grants and other forms of funding;
— The need for federal agencies to support research that is carried out as a joint venture on the part of researchers and practitioners.

The question of whether or not the objectives of the LPA Symposium were attained remains to be seen. It is hoped that the papers presented in the four volumes will add new insights into the issue of language proficiency assessment. It is believed that the research and theoretical perspectives offered will represent a positive step toward attaining the development of effective language proficiency assessment procedures and, ultimately, a more equitable education for language minority students in the United States.

Charlene Rivera

former ALPBP Project Director
Visiting Scholar
NAEP Project
Educational Testing Service

Introduction

This volume grew out of a dialogue between Jim Cummins and other scholars and practitioners present at the Language Proficiency Assessment Symposium. It represents a state of the art discussion of Cummins' theoretical framework.

Cummins first summarizes and explains the development of his theoretical framework relating language proficiency and academic achievement. Five distinguished researchers then, provide critiques which highlight varied perspectives on the long term meaning and implications of Cummins' work. Finally, Cummins responds to the critiques in an attempt to clarify his position.

In the opening chapter, Cummins presents the thesis that,

"a major reason for the confused state of the art of language assessment in bilingual programs ... stems from the failure to develop an adequate theoretical framework for relating language proficiency to academic achievement."

Based on this rationale, Cummins describes the evolution of his theoretical framework. Two premises — the threshold and interdependence hypotheses — form the foundation of the framework. Both theoretical and practical considerations, he contends, influenced the distinction between "basic interpersonal communication skills (BICS) and cognitive — academic language proficiency (CALP)". On a theoretical level, the difference between " 'surface fluency' and more cognitively and academically related aspects of language profieicncy" lead to this differentiation; and on a practical level, the state of the art of "language proficiency assessment techniques ... and procedures for exiting students from bilingual programs", made the demarcation necessary. However, he notes, because the distinctions have been misinterpreted, he will avoid use of the acronyms BICS and CALP, although their underlying meaning within the framework remains the same.

In describing the model for the framework, he emphasizes the importance of its ability to account for developmental and individual differences, as well as its capability to allow for the developmental relationship between first and second language proficiency. He acknowledges that although the framework has need for empirical confirmation, it "appears to permit the complexity of L1–L2 relationships to be conceptualized at the same time as it provides a more adequate rationale . . . that academic skills in L1 and L2 are interdependent".

Fred Genesee acknowledges that the framework proposed by Cummins is important both theoretically and practically. However, he cautions, that because it is based primarily on cognitive and linguistic considerations it lacks a "serious and detailed understanding of the broader social context in which language development and use occur". His criticisms stem from an examination of the "underlying nature of the different language proficiencies . . . their development relationship . . . and the application of the model in educational decision making". He indicates that although Cummins has made a valuable contribution to understanding the relationship between language proficiency and academic achievement, it would be premature to use the framework "to develop test programs, or even bilingual curricula on the basis of these putative language proficiencies without understanding their relationship with more fundamental causal factors."

Like Genesee, Michael Canale concludes that Cummins has made a valuable contribution to the understanding of language proficiency. In its present form, however, he finds that the framework lacks clarity with regard to classification tasks, the relevant features required for contextual support and the developmental sequence required to operationalize the framework. Moreover, he points out it fails to distinguish among:

— basic;
— communicative; and
— autonomous

aspects of language proficiency.

In an attempt to respond to these inadequacies, he delineates the features of a new working theoretical "hypothesis". Although not fully detailed, Canale suggests that, unlike Cummins' framework, his is capable of handling the three identified critical aspects of language proficiency and that, more importantly, it provides a working framework which can address important language testing research issues such as validity and test interpretation.

In the next chapter, Spolsky questions Cummins' naming of factors which are not yet fully identifiable. Specifically, he criticizes Cummins' use of the terms "basic interpersonal communicative skills" and "cognitive academic language proficiency" which he finds to be highly value loaded and "egregious examples of misleading labeling". He suggests that when the terms are reduced to the acronyms — BICS and CALP — they not only increase vagueness but more seriously, set up a false dichotomy which may be socially dangerous. He acknowledges Cummins' willingness to reconsider the use of the acronyms and indicates that this position will, no doubt, in the long run facilitate overall understanding of the factors defined in the framework and of the framework itself.

Rudolph Troike considers another aspect of the sociocultural context, or lack thereof, in Cummins' framework. He theorizes that cultural and social factors rather than linguistic factors may account for most of the disparities in academic achievement among minority students and that for this reason the CALP factor may be merely an indicator of a student's acculturation rather than a cognitive ability. He indicates that while there is little understanding of the "ways home background, including SES", influence the learner, there is even less of an understanding of how "sociolinguistic/cultural attitudes, expectations, and behaviors manifested by the teacher and others" interact to stimulate or retard the individual learner's progress. Because these factors are largely unaccounted for in Cummin's hypotheses, and may only "reveal aculturative approximations to middle-class western cultural norms and behaviors," Troike concludes that much more empirical research into social, cultural, individual and linguistic factors is needed before an adequate model describing the relationship between language proficiency and academic achievement can be achieved.

Benji Wald, like Troike, is concerned with the strengths and weakness of the framework from a sociolinguistic perspective. He indicates that the "framework has proven to be both powerful in its durability and responsive to sociolinguistic considerations". However, he predicts that it will remain an "academic abstraction" unless concepts in the framework are refined and clarified to be reflective of the sociocultural/sociolinguistic realities of language minority students.

In the final chapter Cummins attempts to clarify the "perception that the role of social factors in explaining differential school success has been neglected in comparison to the role assigned to cognitive/linguistic factors". In general, he acknowledges the need for empirical research to clarify theoretical aspects of the framework. Finally, he addresses concerns raised by individual authors.

This interdisciplinary dialogue raises important issues of concern not only to researchers but to educational practitioners and clinicians at all levels. As such, it is hoped that the knowledge gained from the interaction represented in this volume leads to greater theoretical and practical understanding of the critical areas related to language proficiency assessment.

Wanted: A theoretical framework for relating language proficiency to academic achievement among bilingual students[1]

Jim Cummins
The Ontario Institute for Studies in Education

It is argued in the present paper that a major reason for the confused state of the art of language proficiency assessment in bilingual programs (and indeed for the confusion surrounding the rationale for bilingual education) stems from the failure to develop an adequate theoretical framework for relating language proficiency to academic achievement. Without such a theoretical framework it is impossible either to develop rational entry and exit criteria for bilingual programs or to design testing procedures to assess these criteria. Before elaborating the present theoretical framework, an outline of the evolution of its central tenets will be presented. The purpose of this is two-fold: first, to illustrate how the construct of "language proficiency" is central to a variety of seemingly independent issues in the education of language minority and majority students; and second, to help clarify how the present framework is related to theoretical constructs elaborated in previous papers.

Evolution of the Theoretical Framework

Consideration of the apparently contradictory influences of bilingualism on cognitive and academic functioning reported in research literature gave rise to an initial hypothesis regarding the relationship between bilingual skills and cognition. Based on the fact that the development of age-appropriate proficiency in two languages appeared to be associated with cognitive advantages, whereas the attainment of only relatively low levels of bilingual proficiency was associated with cognitive disadvantages, it was hypothesized that there may be two threshold levels of linguistic proficiency: The first, lower, threshold must be attained by bilingual children in order to avoid cognitive disadvantages and the second, higher, threshold was necessary to allow the potentially beneficial aspects of bilingualism to influence cognitive growth (Cummins, 1976, 1979; Toukomaa & Skutnabb-Kangas, 1977).

The postulation of two thresholds was clearly speculative but the hypothesis has proved useful in interpreting subsequent research findings (e.g. Duncan & DeAvila, 1979; Kessler & Quinn, 1980). One of the issues raised by the hypothesis has recently emerged as a central question in the educational debate about exit criteria in the context of U.S. bilingual programs, namely: "When does a language minority student have sufficient English proficiency (i.e. a threshold level) to participate effectively in an all-English classroom?"

However, the hypothesis did not consider in any depth the nature of the bilingual proficiencies which constituted the "thresholds", except to note that the thresholds would vary according to the linguistic and cognitive demands of the curriculum at different grades. This was considered to be an empirical issue; however, as the continuing debate about exit criteria demonstrates, relevant empirical studies remain to be done.

The threshold hypothesis was intended to provide a framework for predicting the cognitive and academic effects of different forms of bilingualism. However, in its initial formulation (Cummins, 1976), the relationships between the first language (L1) and the second language (L2) proficiencies were not explicitly considered. The threshold hypothesis was later (Cummins, 1978) supplemented by the "interdependence" hypothesis which suggested that L1 and L2 academic proficiencies were developmentally interdependent, i.e. in educational contexts the development of L2 proficiency was *partially* dependent upon the prior level of development of L1 proficiency. Thus, as reported initially by Skutnabb-Kangas & Toukomaa (1976) and replicated in subsequent studies (see Cummins, 1981a, for a review), older immigrant students (10–12 years old), whose academic proficiency (e.g. literacy skills) in L1 was well-established, developed L2 academic proficiency more rapidly than younger immigrant students. They also attained higher levels of L1 academic proficiency.

Following Skutnabb-Kangas & Toukomaa (1976), a distinction was made between L2 "surface fluency" and more cognitively and academically related aspects of language proficiency (Cummins, 1979). Because the literacy skills of many language minority students were considerably below age-appropriate levels, it was suggested that the ability of these students to converse in peer-appropriate ways in everyday face-to-face situations (in both L1 and L2) represented, in some respects, a "linguistic facade" hiding large gaps in academically-related aspects of L1 and L2 proficiency (Cummins, 1979; Skutnabb-Kangas & Toukomaa, 1976). However, it was strongly emphasized that language minority students' educational deficits were a function of inappropriate treatment by the school, and that their basic cognitive abilities and command of the linguistic system of their L1 were in no sense deficient (e.g. Cummins, 1979, p. 240).

In subsequent papers (Cummins, 1980a, 1980b) these two aspects of language proficiency were referred to as "basic interpersonal communicative skills" (BICS) and "cognitive-academic language proficiency" (CALP). The distinction was formalized in this way in order to facilitate communication to practitioners involved in educating language minority students. As outlined later in this paper, the failure of educators to take account of this distinction was (and is) actively contributing to the academic failure of language minority students. For example, because students appear to be able to converse easily in English, psychologists often consider it appropriate to administer an individual norm-referenced verbal IQ (CALP) test. Similarly, students are frequently exited from bilingual classrooms on the assumption that because they have attained apparently fluent English face-to-face communicative skills, they are, therefore, "English proficient" and capable of surviving in an all-English classroom.

The CALP-BICS distinction was *not* a distinction between "communicative" and "cognitive" aspects of language proficiency. It was emphasized (Cummins, 1980b) that BICS referred only to some salient rapidly developed aspects of communicative proficiency and that children's social and pragmatic communicative skills encompassed much more than the relatively superficial aspects (e.g. accent, fluency, etc.) upon which educators frequently based their intuitive judgements of language minority students' English proficiency. Similarly, it was stressed that CALP was socially grounded and could only develop within a matrix of human interaction.

Within the framework of the CALP-BICS distinction, the interdependence hypothesis was reformulated in terms of the "common underlying proficiency" (CUP) model of bilingual proficiency in which CALP in L1 and L2 (e.g. reading skills) were regarded as manifestations of one underlying dimension (Cummins, 1980b, 1981a). This common underlying proficiency is theoretically capable of being developed through instruction in either language. Thus, instruction in Spanish in a U.S. bilingual program for language minority students or instruction in French in a Canadian French immersion program for majority students is not developing only Spanish or

French academic skills: it is also developing the general cognitive and academic abilities which underlie English achievement; hence, the rapid transfer of literacy skills across languages observed in these programs. Whether or not instruction in a particular language (L1 or L2) will successfully develop CALP will depend on sociocultural factors as much as pedagogical factors (Cummins, 1980b).

In the present chapter, the distinction that was made between CALP and BICS is elaborated into a theoretical framework for relating language proficiency to academic achievement among bilingual students. The terms "CALP" and "BICS" are not used because of concerns expressed about possible misinterpretation of their meaning and implications. However, the basic distinctions highlighted by these terms are unchanged. The necessity to make such distinctions can be illustrated by the confused state of the art of language proficiency assessment in bilingual programs.

Language Proficiency Assessment in Bilingual Programs

A cursory examination of the many tests of language proficiency and dominance currently available for assessing bilingual students (see, e.g. DeAvila & Duncan, 1978; Dieterich, Freeman & Crandall, 1979) reveals enormous variation in what they purport to measure. Of the 46 tests examined by DeAvila & Duncan (1978), only four included a measure of phoneme production, 43 claimed to measure various levels of lexical ability, 34 included items assessing oral syntax comprehension and nine attempted to assess pragmatic aspects of language.

This variation in language tests is not surprising in view of the lack of consensus as to the nature of language proficiency or "communicative competence". For example, Hernandez-Chavez, Burt & Dulay (1978) have outlined a model of language proficiency comprising 64 separate components, each of which, hypothetically at least, is independently measurable. By contrast, Oller & Perkins (1980) have argued that:

"a single factor of global language proficiency seems to account for the lion's share of variance in a wide variety of educational tests including nonverbal *and* verbal IQ measures, achievement batteries, and even personality inventories and affective measures... the results to date are... preponderantly in favor of the assumption that language skill pervades every area of the school curriculum even more strongly than was ever thought by curriculum writers or testers" (p. 1).

This global dimension is not regarded by Oller (1981) as the only significant factor in language proficiency, but the amount of additional variance accounted for by other factors is relatively modest.

The considerable evidence that Oller and his colleagues (e.g. Oller & Perkins, 1980) have assembled to show that academic and cognitive variables are strongly related to at least some measures of all four general language skills (i.e. listening, speaking, reading and writing) raises an important issue for the assessment of entry and exit criteria in bilingual programs: To what extent *should* measures of language proficiency be related to measures of academic achievement? In other words, to what extent does the construct of language proficiency overlap with the constructs of "intelligence" and academic achievement?

This theoretical question has rarely been asked; instead, researchers have either asked only the empirical question of how language proficiency *is* related to achievement (often expressed in terms of the relation between "oral language" and reading) or else ignored the issue entirely, presumably because they do not consider it relevant to language proficiency assessment in bilingual education. However, the theoretical issue cannot be avoided. The relationship of language proficiency to academic achievement must be considered in view of the fact that a central purpose in assessing minority students' language dominance patterns is to assign students to classes taught in the language through which, it is assumed, they are most capable of learning, and in which they will most readily acquire academic skills. If measures of language proficiency bear no relationship to students' acquisition of academic skills, their relevance in the context of entry and exit criteria is open to question. This issue requires theoretical rather than empirical resolution because, as will be discussed below, some language measures correlate highly with achievement while others show a negligible relationship. Without a theoretical framework within which language proficiency can be related to the development of academic skills there is no basis for choosing between alternative tests which are clearly measuring very different things under the guise of "language proficiency."

Essentially, what is at issue are the criteria to be used in determining the validity of language proficiency measures in the specific context of bilingual education. Whether we are talking about content, criterion-referenced, construct, face, or ecological validity, our procedures for determining validity are always based on a theory regarding the nature of the phenomenon being measured. In many cases, however, this theory has remained implicit in language test development for bilingual students and, where the theory has been made explicit, the construct of language proficiency has usually been regarded as independent of the constructs of intellectual and academic abilities.

Thus, it is reported (see Oakland, 1977, p. 199) that on the *Basic*

Language Competence Battery (Cervenka, 1972) there is little or no increase in scores across the elementary grades among native speakers. This is interpreted as evidence for the construct validity of the battery in that it is indeed measuring "language knowledge" rather than intellectual abilities or educational achievement. In arguing against "language deficit" theories, many sociolinguists (e.g. Labov, 1969; Shuy, 1979) have similarly asserted that language proficiency is independent of cognitive and academic performance. Shuy (1979, p. 5), for example, states that "rather compelling evidence rejects every claim made by those who attempt to show linguistic correlates of cognitive deficit".

One apparent implication of the theoretical position that "language proficiency" is independent of intellectual abilities and academic achievement is that language measures such as the integrative tests (e.g. oral cloze, dictation, elicited imitation) used in the research of Oller and others (see Oller & Perkins, 1980) would have to be rejected as invalid to assess the construct of "language proficiency" because of their strong relationships to achievement and IQ.[2]

Many theorists would regard any form of contrived test situation as inadequate to assess language proficiency, arguing instead for procedures which assess children's language in naturally-occurring communicative situations (e.g. Cazden, Bond, Epstein, Matz, & Savignon, 1977; Dieterich *et al.*, 1979). For example, Dieterich *et al.* (1979) argue in relation to an elicited imitation task that "it mirrors no real speech situation and is thus of questionable validity in assessing proficiency" (p. 541).

Although the requirement that proficiency measures reflect "naturally-occurring speech situations" is a basic principle of validity for many theorists, few pursue the issue to inquire whether or not the communicative demands of natural face-to-face situations are identical to the communicative demands of classroom situations. In classrooms, a student's opportunity to negotiate meaning with the interlocutor (teacher) is considerably reduced as a result of sharing him or her with about 25–30 other students. There is also considerable emphasis on developing proficiency in processing written text where the meaning is supported largely by linguistic cues rather than the richer "real-life" cues of face-to-face communication.

These issues are being raised not to argue against the assessment of "language proficiency" in naturally-occurring situations but rather to show the need for a theoretical framework which would allow the construct of language proficiency to be conceptualized in relation to the acquisition of academic skills in bilingual programs. The urgency of this need can be seen from the fact that the most commonly-used tests of language proficiency and dominance for minority students clearly embody different theoretical assumptions in regard to the relationship between language proficiency and achievement. The *Language Assessment Scales (LAS)* (DeAvila & Duncan, 1977), for example, are reported to consistently show moderate correlations with academic achievement whereas the *Bilingual Syntax Measure (BSM)* (Burt, Dulay, & Hernandez-Chevez, 1975) and the *Basic Inventory of Natural Language (BINL)* (Herbert, 1977) tend to show much lower correlations with achievement (see Rosansky, 1981, for a review). All of these tests showed lower correlations with achievement than teachers' ratings of students' chances for academic achievement if instructed only in English (Ulibarri, Spencer & Rivas, 1981). This teacher variable accounted for 41% of the variance in reading achievement scores and the BINL, BSM and LAS added only zero, one and four per cent respectively to the prediction of reading achievement.

Apart from the issue of their relationship to academic achievement, the validity of these tests can be questioned on several other grounds. For example, Rosansky (1979) points out that data elicited by the BSM-English were unrelated to data elicited from taped naturalistic conversation of the same individuals. The *LAS* Spanish language classification is reported to considerably underestimate the Spanish proficiency of native Spanish speakers as assessed by either teacher ratings or detailed ethnolinguistic analysis of children's speech in a range of settings (Mace-Matluck, 1980).

This brief survey of assessment issues in bilingual education suggests that a major reason for the confused state of the art is that the developmental relationships between language proficiency (in L1 and L2) and academic performance have scarcely been considered, let alone resolved. The confusion about the assessment of "language proficiency" is reflected in the varied criteria used to exit language minority students from bilingual programs.

"English Proficiency" and Exit Criteria

Lack of English proficiency is commonly regarded by policy makers and educators as the major cause of language minority students' academic failure in English-only programs. Thus, it is assumed that students require bilingual instruction only until they have become proficient in English. Logically, after students have become "proficient in English", any difficulties they might encounter in an English-only program cannot be attributed to lack of English proficiency.

If we combine this apparent logic with the fact that immigrant students generally appear to acquire a reasonably high level of L2 fluency within about one-and-a-half to two years of arrival in the host country (Cummins, in press; Snow & Hoefnagel-Höhle, 1978), then one might assume that two years of bilingual education should be sufficient for students to make the transition to an English-only program. This line of reasoning is frequently invoked to justify exiting students out of bilingual programs after a relatively short period. It is assumed that, because students can cope adequately with the communicative demands of face-to-face situations and may appear quite fluent in English, therefore their English proficiency is sufficiently well-developed to cope with the communicative demands of the regular English-only curriculum on an equal basis with native English-speaking students.

There is considerable evidence to suggest that this logic is false. Bilingual programs which have been successful in developing a high level of English academic skills in language minority students have usually maintained instruction in L1 throughout elementary school. Usually it is only in the later grades of elementary school that students approach grade norms in English reading skills (see Cummins, 1981a, for a review). In a similar way, it has been shown (Cummins, 1981b) that it took immigrant students who arrived in Canada after the age of six, 5–7 years, on the average, to approach grade norms in academically-related aspects of English proficiency. Thus, it clearly takes considerably longer for language minority students to develop age-appropriate *academic* skills in English than it does to develop certain aspects of age-appropriate English face-to-face communicative skills. It follows that students exited on the basis of teacher judgements or language tests which primarily assess face-to-face communicative skills are likely to experience considerable academic difficulty in an English-only program, and many will manifest the well-documented pattern of cumulative deficits.

The dangers of unanalysed notions of what constitutes "English proficiency" can be illustrated by an example from a Canadian study in which the teacher referral forms and psychological assessments of 428 language minority students were analysed (Cummins, in press). This particular child (PR) was first referred in grade 1 by the school principal who noted that:

"PR is experiencing considerable difficulty with grade 1 work. An intellectual assessment would help her teacher to set realistic learning expectations for her and might provide some clues as to remedial assistance that might be offered."

No mention was made of the child's English-as-a-second-language (ESL) background; this only emerged when the child was referred by the grade two teacher in the following year. Thus, the psychologist does not consider this as a possible factor in accounting for the discrepancy between a Verbal IQ of 64 and a Performance IQ of 108. The assessment report read as follows:

> "Although overall ability level appears to be within the low average range, note the significant difference between verbal and nonverbal scores. . . . It would appear that PR's development has not progressed at a normal rate and consequently she is, and will continue to experience much difficulty in school. Teacher's expectations (at this time) should be set accordingly."

What is interesting in this example is that the child's face-to-face communicative skills are presumably sufficiently well-developed that the psychologist (and possibly the teacher) is not alerted to her ESL background. This leads the psychologist to infer from her low verbal IQ score that "her development has not progressed at a normal rate" and to advise the teacher to set low academic expectations for the child since she "will continue to experience much difficulty in school". There is ample evidence from many contexts (e.g. Mercer, 1973) of how the attribution of deficient cognitive skills to language minority students can become self-fulfilling.

In many of the referral forms and psychological assessments analysed in this study the following line of reasoning was invoked:

> Because language minority students are fluent in English, their poor academic performance and/or test scores cannot be attributed to lack of proficiency in English. Therefore, these students must either have deficient cognitive abilities or be poorly motivated ('lazy').

In a similar way, when language minority students are exited from bilingual programs on the basis of fluent English communicative skills, it appears that their subsequent academic difficulties cannot logically be attributed to "lack of English proficiency". Thus, educators are likely to attribute these difficulties to factors within the student such as "low academic ability" (IQ).

These misconceptions derive from the fact that the relationships between "language proficiency" and academic development have not been adequately considered, either among native English-speaking or language minority students. In the remainder of this chapter a theoretical framework is developed for conceptualizing these relationships.

A Theoretical Framework[3]

On the basis of the foregoing analysis of the confusions which exist both in current language proficiency assessment techniques and in procedures for exiting students from bilingual programs, three minimal requirements for a theoretical framework of language proficiency relevant to bilingual education in the United States can be outlined: First, such a framework must incorporate a developmental perspective such that those aspects of language proficiency which are mastered early by native speakers and L2 learners can be distinguished from those that continue to vary across individuals as development progresses; Second, the framework must be capable of allowing differences between the linguistic demands of the school and those of interpersonal contexts outside the school to be described; Third, the framework must be capable of allowing the developmental relationships between L1 and L2 proficiency to be described.

Current theoretical frameworks of "communicative competence" (e.g. Canale & Swain, 1980; Canale, 1981) do not and were not intended to meet these requirements. Canale (1981) distinguishes grammatical, sociolinguistic, discourse and strategic competencies but states that their relationships with each other and with knowledge of the world and academic achievement is an empirical question yet to be addressed. Although this framework is extremely useful for some purposes, its applicability to bilingual education is limited by its static nondevelopmental nature and by the fact that the relationships between academic performance and the components of communicative competence in L1 and L2 are not considered. For example, both pronunciation and lexical knowledge would both be classified under grammatical competence. Yet, L1 pronunciation is mastered very early by native speakers, whereas lexical knowledge continues to develop throughout schooling and is strongly related to academic performance.

The framework outlined below is an attempt to conceptualize "language proficiency" in such a way that the developmental interrelationships between academic performance and language proficiency in both L1 and L2 can be considered. It is proposed only in relation to the development of academic skills in bilingual education and is not necessarily appropriate or applicable to other contexts or issues. Essentially, the framework tries to integrate the earlier distinction between basic interpersonal communicative skills (BICS) and cognitive/academic language proficiency (CALP) into a more general theoretical model. The BICS–CALP distinction was intended to make the same point that was made earlier in this paper, namely, academic deficits are often created by teachers and psychologists who fail to realize that it takes language minority students considerably longer to attain grade/age-appropriate levels in English academic skills than it does in English face-to-face communicative skills. However, as is pointed out in other papers in this volume, such a dichotomy oversimplifies the phenomena and risks misinterpretation. It is also difficult to discuss the crucial developmental issues in terms of the BICS-CALP dichotomy.

The framework presented in Figure 1 proposes that in the context of bilingual education in the United States "language proficiency" can be conceptualized along two continuums. The first is a continuum relating to

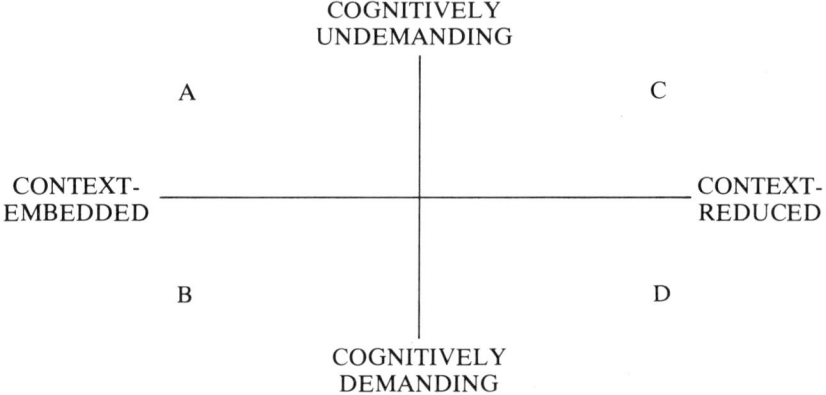

FIGURE 1   Range of Contextual Support and Degree of Cognitive Involvement in Communicative Activities.

the range of contextual support available for expressing or receiving meaning. The extremes of this continuum are described in terms of "context-embedded" versus "context-reduced" communication. They are distinguished by the fact that in context-embedded communication the particpants can actively negotiate meaning (e.g. by providing feedback that the message has not been understood) and the language is supported by a wide range of meaningful paralinguistic and situational cues. Context-reduced communication, on the other hand relies primarily (or at the extreme of the continuum, exclusively) on linguistic cues to meaning and may in some cases involve suspending knowledge of the "real world" in order to interpret (or manipulate) the logic of the communication appropriately.[4]

In general, context-embedded communication derives from interpersonal involvement in a shared reality which obviates the need for explicit linguistic elaboration of the message. Context-reduced communication, on the other hand, derives from the fact that this shared reality cannot be assumed, and thus linguistic messages must be elaborated precisely and explicitly so that the risk of misinterpretation is minimized. It is important to emphasize that this is a continuum and not a dichotomy. Thus, examples of communicative behaviors going from left to right along the continuum might be: engaging in a discussion, writing a letter to a close friend, writing (or reading) an academic article. Clearly, context-embedded communication is more typical of the everyday world outside the classroom, whereas many of the linguistic demands of the classroom reflect communication which is closer to the context-reduced end of the continuum.

The vertical continuum is intended to address the developmental aspects of communicative proficiency in terms of the degree of active cognitive involvement in the task or activity. Cognitive involvement can be conceptualized in terms of the amount of information that must be processed simultaneously or in close succession by the individual in order to carry out the activity.

How does this continuum incorporate a developmental perspective? If we return to the four components of communicative competence (grammatical, sociolinguistic, discourse, and strategic) discussed by Canale (1981) it is clear that within each one, some subskills (e.g. pronunciation and syntax within L1 grammatical competence) reach plateau levels at which there are no longer significant differences in mastery between individuals (at least in context-embedded situations). Other subskills continue to develop throughout the school years and beyond, depending upon the individual's communicative needs in particular cultural and institutional milieux.

Thus, the upper parts of the vertical continuum consist of communicative tasks and activities in which the linguistic tools have become largely automatized (mastered) and thus require little active cognitive involvement for appropriate performance. At the lower end of the continuum are tasks and activities in which the communicative tools have not become automatized and thus require active cognitive involvement. Persuading another individual that your point of view rather than her/his is correct, or writing an essay on a complex theme are examples of such activities. In these situations, it is necessary to stretch one's linguistic resources (i.e. grammatical, sociolinguistic, discourse and strategic competences) to the limit in order to achieve one's communicative goals. Obviously, cognitive involvement, in the sense of amount of information processing, can be just as intense in context-embedded as in context-reduced activities.

As mastery is developed, specific linguistic tasks and skills travel from the bottom towards the top of the vertical continuum. In other words, there tends to be a high level of cognitive involvement in task or activity performance until mastery has been achieved or, alternatively, until a plateau level at less than mastery levels has been reached (e.g. L2 pronunciation in many adult immigrants, "fossilization" of certain grammatical features among French immersion students, etc.). Thus, learning the phonology and syntax of L1, for example, requires considerable cognitive involvement for the two and three year old child, and therefore these tasks would be placed in quadrant B (context-embedded, cognitively demanding). However, as mastery of these skills develops, tasks involving them would move from quadrant B to quadrant A since performance becomes increasingly automatized and cognitively undemanding. In a second language context the same type of developmental progression occurs.

The third requirement for a theoretical framework applicable to bilingual education is that it permits the developmental interrelationships between L1 and L2 proficiency to be conceptualized. There is considerable evidence that L1 and L2 proficiency are interdependent, i.e. manifestations of a common underlying proficiency (see Cummins, 1981a). The evidence reviewed in support of the interdependence hypothesis primarily involved academic or "context-reduced" language proficiency because the hypothesis was developed explicitly in relation to the development of bilingual academic skills. However, any language task which is cognitively-demanding for a group of individuals is likely to show a moderate degree of interdependence across languages. Also, other factors (e.g. personality, learning style, etc.), in addition to general cognitive skills, are likely to contribute to the relationship between L1 and L2 and thus some cognitively-undemanding aspects of proficiency (e.g. fluency) may also be related across languages.

As far as context-reduced language proficiency is concerned, the transferability across languages of many of the proficiencies involved in reading (e.g. inferring and predicting meaning based on sampling from the text) and writing (e.g. planning large sections of discourse) is obvious. However, even where the task-demands are language-specific (e.g. decoding or spelling) a strong relationship may be obtained between skills in L1 and L2 as a result of a more generalized proficiency (and motivation) to handle cognitively-demanding context-reduced language tasks. Similarly, on the context-embedded side, many sociolinguistic rules of face-to-face communication are language-specific, but L1 and L2 sociolinguistic skills may be related as a result of a possible generalized sensitivity to sociolinguistic rules of discourse.

In conclusion, the theoretical framework appears to permit the complexity of L1-L2 relationships to be conceptualized at the same time as it provides a more adequate rationale for the essentially simple point that academic skills in L1 and L2 are interdependent. The framework also provides the basis for a task-analysis of measures of "language proficiency" which would allow the relationships between language measures and academic performance to be predicted for any particular group of individuals. In general, the more context-reduced and cognitively-demanding the language task, the more it will be related to achievement. However, although there are intrinsic characteristics of some language tasks which make them more cognitively-demanding and context-reduced, these task characteristics must be considered in conjunction with the characteristics of the particular language users (e.g. L1 and/or L2 proficiency, learning style, etc.). For example, skills that have become automatized for native speakers of a language may very well be highly cognitively-demanding for learners of that language as an L2. Thus, one would expect different relationships between achievement and certain language tasks in an L1 as compared to an L2 context.[5]

Assessment of Entry and Exit Criteria Revisited

The theoretical framework can readily be applied to the issue of the assessment of entry and exit criteria. The problem highlighted earlier was that language minority students often manifest proficiencies in some context-embedded aspects of English (quadrant A) and are, consequently, regarded as having sufficient "English proficiency" both to follow a regular English curriculum and to take psychological and educational tests in English. What is not realized by many educators is that because of language minority students' ESL background, the regular English curriculum and psychological assessment procedures are considerably more context-reduced and cognitively-demanding than they are for English-background students. In other words, students' English proficiency may not be sufficiently developed to cope with communicative demands which are very different from those of face-to-face situations.

What assessment procedures should be used for entry and exit in bilingual programs? Given that the purpose of language proficiency assessment in bilingual education is *placement* of students in classes taught through the language which, it is assumed, will best promote the development of academic skills, it is necessary that the procedures assess proficiencies related to the communicative demands of schooling. However, in order to be valid, the procedures should also reflect children's previous experience with language. Because the child's language experiences prior to school have been largely in context-embedded situations, the assessment procedures for entry purposes should involve cognitively-demanding context-embedded measures which are fair to the variety of L1 (and L2) spoken by the child. However, for exit purposes, it is recommended that cognitively-demanding context-reduced measures be used because these more accurately reflect the communicative demands of an all-English classroom. If children are unable to handle the context-reduced demands of an English test, there is little reason to believe that they have developed sufficient "English proficiency" to compete on an equal basis with native English-speaking children in a regular English classroom.

These suggestions derive from a theoretical analysis of the relationships between language proficiency and academic performance and clearly require empirical confirmation. However, without a theoretical framework for conceptualizing these relationships, legitimate empirical questions cannot even be asked. An example of a commonly-posed empirical question which is essentially meaningless when asked in a theoretical vacuum is the issue of the relationship between "oral language proficiency" and reading. Within the context of the present framework "oral language proficiency" could equally refer to cognitively-undemanding context-embedded skills as to cognitively-demanding context-reduced skills. As one would expect on the basis of the present analysis, there is little relationship between these two aspects of "oral language proficiency". Also, reading skills are strongly related to the latter, but unrelated to the former (see e.g. Cummins, 1981a).

In summary, the major reasons for the confusion in regard to assessment procedures for entry and exit criteria in bilingual education is that neither the construct of language proficiency itself, nor its relationship to the development of cognitive and academic skills has been adequately conceptualized. The extreme positions that (1) language proficiency is essentially independent of cognitive and academic skills, implied by some sociolinguists on the basis of ethnographically-oriented research and (2) language proficiency is largely indistinguishable from cognitive and academic skills, suggested by much of the psychometric research reviewed by Oller and his colleagues, both arbitrarily identify particular aspects of the construct of language proficiency with the totality of the construct. In the present paper it has been argued that language proficiency cannot be conceptualized as one static entity or as 64 static entities. It is constantly developing along different dimensions (e.g. grammatical, sociolinguistic, discourse and strategic dimensions) and being specialized for different contexts of use among monolingual English-speaking as well as language minority children. In academic contexts, certain aspects of language proficiency develop in specialized ways to become the major tool for meeting the cognitive and communicative demands of schooling. A major implication of the present framework is that recognition of the very different communicative proficiencies required of children in school encounters as compared to the one-to-one, face-to-face interaction typical of out-of-school contexts is a first step towards the development of theoretically and empirically viable entry and exit procedures.

Notes

1. The need for a theoretical framework explicitly designed to relate language proficiency to academic achievement was brought home to me at the Language Proficiency Assessment Symposium (LPAS) not only as a result of criticisms of the distinction which I had introduced between basic interpersonal communicative skills (BICS) and cognitive/academic language proficiency (CALP) but, more importantly, by the lack of any resolution of the issues to which that distinction was addressed. The present theoretical framework is essentially an elaboration and, hopefully, a clarification of the BICS — CALP distinction. In addition to the many participants at the LPAS who made valuable suggestions, I would like to acknowledge my debt to John Oller Jr. and to Merrill Swain for many useful discussions on these issues.
2. Much of the vehemence with which researchers have rejected the verbal components of standardized IQ and achievement tests as valid measures of either "language proficiency" or cognitive abilities stems from the blatant misuse of such measures with low socioeconomic status (SES) and ethnic minority students (see for example, Cummins, 1980a). However, the fact that SES or cultural differences on such measures can be explained by acculturation to middle-class majority group norms does not account for differences between individuals *within* SES or cultural groups on cognitively-demanding culture-specific measures of proficiency. In other words, it is logically invalid to argue that a particular phenomenon (e.g. cognitive development) does not exist because some of the tools used to measure that phenomenon (e.g. IQ tests) have been abused.
3. This theoretical framework should be viewed within a social context. The language proficiencies described develop as a result of various types of communicative interactions in home and school (see e.g. Wells, 1981). The nature of these interactions is, in turn, determined by broader societal factors (see Cummins, 1981a). In order to emphasize the social nature of "language proficiency", this term will be used interchangeably with "communicative proficiency" in describing the framework.
4. The term "context-reduced" is used rather than "disembedded" (Donaldson 1978) or "decontextualized" because there is a large variety of contextual cues available to carry out tasks even at the context-reduced end of the continuum. The difference, however, is that these cues are exclusively *linguistic* in nature.
5. It should be pointed out that the framework in no way implies that language pedagogy should be context-reduced. There is considerable evidence from both first and second language pedagogy (e.g. Smith, 1978; Swain, 1978) to support the principle that context-reduced language proficiency can be most successfully developed on the basis of initial instruction which maximizes the degree of

context-embeddedness. In other words, the more instruction is in tune with the experience and skills the child brings to school (i.e. the more meaningful it is), the more learning will occur. This is one of the reasons why bilingual education is, in general, more successful for language minority students than English-only programs.

References

Burt, M., Dulay, H. & Hernandez-Chavez, E. 1975, *Bilingual syntax measure*. New York: Harcourt, Brace, Jovanovitch.
Canale, M. 1981, From communicative competence to communicative language pedagogy. In J. Richards & R. Schmidt (eds), *Language and communication*. Manuscript submitted for publication.
Canale, M., & Swain, M. 1980, Theoretical bases of communicative approaches to second language teaching and testing. *Applied Linguistics*, 1(1), 1–47.
Cazden, C., Bond, J., Epstein, A., Matz, R. & Savignon, J. 1977, Language assessment: Where, what and how. *Anthropology and Education Quarterly*, 8(2), 83–91.
Cervenka, E. J. 1972, *Basic Language Competence Battery*, New York: E. J. Cervenka.
Cummins, J. 1976, The influence of bilingualism on cognitive growth: A synthesis of research findings and explanatory hypotheses. *Working Papers on Bilingualism*, 9, 1–43.
— 1978, Educational implications of mother tongue maintenance in minority-language groups. *The Canadian Modern Language Review*, 34, 395–416.
— 1979, Linguistic interdependence and the educational development of bilingual children. *Review of Educational Research*, 49(2), 222–51.
— 1980a, The cross-lingual dimensions of language proficiency: Implications for bilingual education and the optimal age issue. *TESOL Quarterly*, 14, 175–87.
— 1980b, The entry and exit fallacy in bilingual education. *NABE Journal*, 4(3), 25–60.
— 1981a, The role of primary language development in promoting educational success for language minority students. In California State Department of Education, *Schooling and language minority students: A theoretical framework*, Los Angeles: Evaluation, Dissemination and Assessment Center.
— 1981b, Age on arrival and immigrant second language learning in Canada: A reassessment. *Applied Linguistics*, 2(2), 132–49.
— in press, *Bilingualism and special education: Issues in assessment and pedagogy*. Clevedon, Avon: Multilingual Matters.
DeAvila, E. A. & Duncan, S. E. 1977, *Language assessment scales — LAS I & II* (2nd ed.). Corte Madera, CA: Linguametrics Group, Inc.
— 1978, A few thoughts about language assessment: The LAU decision reconsidered. *Bilingual Education Paper Series*, National Dissemination and Assessment Center, 1(8).
Dieterich, T. G., Freeman, C. & Crandall, J. A. 1979, A linguistic analysis of some English proficiency tests. *TESOL Quarterly*, 13(4), 535–50.
Donaldson, M. 1978, *Children's minds*. New York: Norton.
Duncan, S. E. & DeAvila, E. A. 1979, Bilingualism and cognition: Some recent findings. *NABE Journal*, 4(1), 15–50.
Herbert, C. H. 1977, *Basic inventory of natural language* (BINL). San Bernadino, CA: Checkpoint Systems.

Hernandez-Chavez, E., Burt, M. & Dulay, H. 1978, Language dominance and proficiency testing: Some general considerations. *NABE Journal*, 3, 41–54.

Kessler, C. & Quinn, M. E. 1980, Positive effects of bilingualism on science problem-solving abilities. In J. E. Atlatis (ed.), *31st Annual Georgetown University Round Table on Languages and Linguistics.* Washington, D.C.: Georgetown University Press.

Labov, W. 1969, *The study of nonstandard English.* Champaign, Illinois: National Council of Teachers of English.

Mace-Matluck, B. J. 1980, *A longitudinal study of the oral language development of Texas bilingual children (Spanish-English): Findings from the first year.* Paper presented at the National Conference in the Language Arts in the Elementary School, San Antonio, Texas. March.

Mercer, J. 1973, *Labelling the mentally retarded.* Berkeley: University of California Press, 1973.

Oakland, T. 1977, *Psychological and educational assessment of minority children.* New York: Brunner/Mazel.

Oller, Jr., J. W., 1981, Language testing research (1979–80). In R. Kaplan, R. L. Jones & G. R. Tucker (eds), *Annual Review of Applied Linguistics.* Volume I. Rowley, Mass: Newbury House.

Oller, Jr., J. W. & Perkins, K. 1980. *Research in language testing.* Rowley, Mass.: Newbury House.

Rosansky, E. J. 1979, Review of the bilingual syntax measure. In B. Spolsky (ed.), *Some major tests: Advances in language testing: Series: 1.* Arlington, VA: Center for Applied Linguistics.

— 1981, *Future perspectives on research in oral language proficiency assessment.* Paper presented at the InterAmerica Symposium on Language Proficiency Assessment, Airlie House, Virginia, March.

Shuy, R. W. 1979, On the relevance of recent developments in sociolinguistics to the study of language learning and early education. *NABE Journal*, 4, 51–71.

Skutnabb-Kangas, T. & Toukomaa, P. 1976, *Teaching migrant children's mother tongue and learning the language of the host country in the context of the socio-cultural situation of the migrant family.* Tampere, Finland: University of Tampere. (Department of Sociology and Social Psychology Research Report, 15, Box 601.)

Smith, F. 1978, *Understanding reading* (2nd ed.). New York: Holt, Rinehart and Winston.

Snow, C. E. & Hoefnagel-Höhle, M. 1978, The critical period for language acquisition: Evidence from second language learning. *Child Development*, 49, 1114–1128.

Swain, M. 1978, French immersion: Early, late or partial? *The Canadian Modern Language Review*, 34, 577–85.

Toukomaa, P. & Skutnabb-Kangas, T. 1977, *The intensive teaching of the mother tongue to migrant children of pre-school age and children in the lower level of comprehensive school.* Tampere, Finland: University of Tampere. (Department of Sociology and Social Psychology Research Report, 15, Box 601.)

Ulibarri, D., Spencer, M. & Rivas, G. 1981, Language Proficiency and Academic Achievement: A study of language proficiency tests and their relationship to school ratings as predictors of academic achievement. *NABE Journal* 5, 47–80.

Wells, G. 1981, *Learning through interaction: The study of language development.* New York: Cambridge University Press.

On Cummins' theoretical framework

Fred Genesee
McGill University

In "Wanted: A Theoretical Framework for Relating Language Proficiency to Academic Achievement Among Bilingual Students", Cummins (this volume) has attempted to develop a theoretical framework which would account for the success, or lack thereof, of majority and minority language students in different school language programs. The major focus of this framework has been on the relationship between language proficiency, both in the students' native (L1) and second language (L2), and academic achievement. In particular, Cummins has postulated in previous papers that there are two distinct types of language proficiency and that they have differential significance for academic success. One type of language proficiency, called BICS (Basic Interpersonal Communication Skills) is characterized as "cognitively undemanding manifestations of language proficiency in interpersonal situations" (Cummins, 1980, p. 28). The other, called CALP (Cognitive/Academic Language Proficiency) is characterized as cognitively demanding manipulations and interpretations of language which is stripped of extralinguistic supports. It is CALP that is thought to be more highly predictive of academic achievement according to the model, and, therefore, it is CALP that should be the basis of decisions concerning entry to and exit from bilingual school programs.

In the present chapter, Cummins has elaborated the CALP/BICS distinction by differentiating the two major components that comprise these concepts, namely, the extent of context support and of cognitive involvement in language use. An important feature of Cummins' framework, in addition to the distinction just mentioned, is the developmental relationship between the different types of language proficiency, both within each language and between languages. Here Cummins argues that BICS (i.e. context-embedded, cognitively-undemanding use of language) develops more quickly than CALP (i.e. context-reduced, cognitively demanding use of language), and that BICS develops relatively independently in L1 and L2, while L1 and L2 CALP are thought to develop interdependently.

Cummins' postulations are important from both a theoretical and a practical viewpoint since, as he points out himself, such a framework is useful in order to define rational entry and exit criteria for bilingual programs and also presumably in order to develop rational and effective educational programs that will meet the special needs of minority language children. This chapter consists of an examination of Cummins' framework from three perspectives: the first concerns the underlying nature of the different language proficiencies or communicative activities in question and particularly those related to academic contexts; the second concerns their developmental relationship, as just described; and the third concerns the application of the model in educational decision-making.

Language proficiency: its nature

Cummins stresses that the type of language proficiency that is associated with school-related language use, is "socially grounded and could only develop within a matrix of human interaction". However, in subsequent discussions of the relationship between language proficiency and academic achievement, these social foundations are virtually ignored. In fact, Cummins' description of the contrasting conditions, social and cognitive, that characterize academic and non-academic language use gives the impression that social factors are relatively unimportant in the school-related use of language. In particular, he characterizes use of language for academic purposes in terms of high cognitive involvement and reduction of contextual support, whereas use of language outside school is characterized in terms of low cognitive involvement and much contextual support. Cognitive involvement is defined as "the amount of information that must be processed simultaneously or in close succession by the individual in order to carry out the activity." Use of the terms *cognitive* and *information* might imply to some "not socially relevant". There is in fact no reason to preclude *socially*-relevant information from the definition and, indeed, current approaches in social psychology stress the notion of social *cognitions*. A communicative activity that entails high cognitive involvement might be essentially social in nature if the activity requires processing socially relevant information. Even otherwise routine social activities might require high cognitive involvement on the part of individuals who are unfamiliar with the social parameters of the situation and/or who came from a social milieu where the activity is valued differently. Although Cummins' framework does not explicitly preclude social variables in school-related use of language, in its present form it is somewhat vague and, consequently, perhaps misleading on this point. Similarly, the definition of contextual support might inadvertently connote a distinction between social and non-social communicative activities. According to Cummins, "context-embedded communication derives from interpersonal involvement in a shared reality which obviates the need for explicit linguistic elaboration of the message", whereas context-reduced communication occurs when a "shared reality cannot be assumed, and thus linguistic messages must be elaborated precisely and explicitly so that the risk of misinterpretation is minimized". That there is no or little interpersonal involvement in a shared reality during context-reduced communication as there is in context-embedded communication does not mean that the communication takes place in a social vacuum. Certain sociolinguistic conventions characterize the academic use of language just as they do the obviously interpersonal uses of language. Indeed, the importance of these conventions may be just as or more important in the former contexts precisely because they must be expressed formally and unequivocally.

Cole and his colleagues have shown that even such apparently disembedded linguistic tasks as memorizing a list of words are not immune from the effects of social meaning (Cole, Gay, Glick & Sharp, 1971). They found that Kpelle rice farmers and school children in Liberia demonstrated limited verbal memory for lists of isolated words, that they failed to use semantic categories to organize recall; and that they showed no or little improvement in recall with repeated exposure to the lists. In contrast, American subjects demonstrated better overall recall, use of semantic categories for organization of recall, and improvement with successive exposures. Attempts to improve the Kpelles' performance using standard North American experimental manipulations, such as offering incentives, extending the number of trials and showing the objects to be remembered, all failed. However, when the same lists of words were presented in the context of folk stories, the Kpelle subjects showed improvement on all aspects of the task. Cole concluded that situational factors, that in this case were also culturally distinct, were instrumental in producing the results they found. That is to say, the subjects' performance reflected their skill at responding to the social situation posed by the task as much as their verbal memory *per se* (see also Cole & Bruner, 1971).

At issue here is whether one can divorce language use for academic purposes from consideration of social psychology and sociolinguistic variables. The preceding example illustrates, quite clearly, that one cannot. At the same time, some writers have pointed out that language is not invariably used for interpersonal communication. Language may be used for other reasons, including, for example, verbal thinking, problem solving, self-expression and creative writing, (see, for example, Vygotsky, 1962; Canale & Swain, 1980). Cummins' definition appears to focus on these uses of language and to exclude language usage in academic settings that is socially constrained because of the explicitly interpersonal nature of the interaction. What is needed, therefore, is a more balanced treatment such that greater attention is paid to social factors, along with those already articulated by Cummins, in order to arrive at a thorough understanding of the language skills needed to succeed in school.

This is not simply a theoretical issue. Clearly a particular conceptualization of the languge proficiencies under question here will influence measurement of them in specific ways and, as well will determine the kinds of treatments given to students found to be lacking in them. A conceptualization that stresses, or appears to stress, cognitive and/or strictly linguistic dimensions, as do Cummins' definitions, will result in cognitive and/or linguistic tests and treatments.

Language proficiency: its development

Cummins makes the very important general point that any framework that relates language proficiency (proficiencies) to academic achievement "must incorporate a developmental perspective". However, there is a questionable assumption in Cummins' specification that this perspective distinguish "those aspects of language proficiency which are mastered early by native speakers and L2 learners from those that continue to vary across individuals as development progresses". The assumption lies in the inference that early language subskill mastery on the one hand is associated with the lack of individual differences whereas later language subskill mastery on the other hand is associated with the presence of such differences. There is no reason to suspect that early mastery of language skills is associated with fewer individual differences than is later mastery. In fact, in a recent publication, Katherine Nelson (1981) reviews empirical evidence of individual differences in early first language acquisition. Moreover, the assumption of such an association ignores commonly occurring variations in the first language of child speakers from different cultural and social class groups. Clarification is needed here to eliminate this confusion.

Elsewhere in the present article, Cummins argues that "it takes language minority students considerably longer to attain grade/age-appropriate levels in English academic skills than it does in English face-to-face communicative skills"; some empirical evidence in support of this claim is presented. This may in fact be true, and, if it is, it has important implications for bilingual education. In particular, the evident rush among some American educators to integrate minority language children into all English programs is likely to result in less successful transitions than if the switch were delayed. At the same time, Cummins offers no suggestions as to why such differential development should characterize these two putative types of language proficiency. He does suggest that language minority children will acquire academic language skills in L2 faster if their L1 academic language skills are more developed. However, even this relationship is not entirely unequivocal in that children with more advanced L1 academic language skills are also likely to be older and, consequently, more cognitively mature in general. It has been found in numerous research studies that older individuals learn second languages faster than younger learners (Genesee, 1981; Krashen, Long & Scarcella, 1979), although younger learners may ultimately acquire higher levels of proficiency than older learners. Thus, it is not clear from the available evidence whether it is simply L1 mastery that predicts L2 mastery in the case of academic language skills or whether age and possibly other factors play a role.

Judging by the academic performance of many majority language children from lower socio-economic backgrounds, it would appear that it is not just minority language children who experience this developmental language lag. The disproportionately high rate of failure among children from working or lower social class backgrounds suggests that a complete understanding of this phenomenon will not be found in an examination of language and/or cognitive variables alone. This claim is underlined further by the documented academic success of some minority language children from certain Asian groups, even when compared to majority group American youngsters. Moreover, Bruck's (1982) finding that majority English-speaking Canadian children with language disabilities benefit from early total immersion programs also suggest that language alone will not explain the types of subgroup differences that are under investigation when we examine the academic performance of minority language children.

An understanding of the causes underlying the developmental lag in the acquisition of academically-related language skills among minority language children, as well as majority language children, is essential if educators are to develop rational educational interventions that will provide all types of students with the academic skills necessary to succeed in school. Delaying the transition from a bilingual program to a mainstream English program in the case of minority language children may increase their chances of success but in a hit-and-miss fashion. In the absence of a rational, focused approach, time alone may be insufficient to provide all minority language children with the requisite skills. It is not clear that the postulation of different types of language proficiencies and of different developmental relationships between language and academic achievement offers the explanatory principles that are needed; rather educators are left with trying to explain one developmental lag, that related to academic language proficiency, instead of another, that related to academic success.

The entry-exit dilemma

Cummins states:

"Given that the purpose of language proficiency assessment in bilingual education is *placement* of students in classes taught through the language which, it is assumed, will best promote the development of academic skills, it is necessary that the procedures assess proficiencies related to the communicative demands of schooling."

In particular he recommends that assessment procedures for entry purposes should involve cognitively-demanding context-embedded measures which are fair to the variety of L1 (and L2) spoken by the child. No specification is given concerning the actual entry decisions that should follow from the use of these types of assessment measures; nor, in fact, is the actual language of testing specified, although the use of L1 for entry testing is hinted at. Thus, it is difficult to know whether children who test high in L1 at entry should be given L1 instruction or whether they should be placed in an all-English program directly. Given Cummins' concern that language proficiency assessment be related to the types of communicative demands of the school, it is also difficult to understand how the use of context-embedded tests that are fair to the variety of L1 spoken by the child and are, therefore, non-school-related will improve placement in school programs which are characterized as context-reduced. This recommendation makes sense if the educational program the child is to enter incorporates some of the contextual supports the child has had outside school. This would require more than simply using the child's L1 as the medium of instruction. Furthermore, how do the cognitive abilities associated with extracurricular context-embedded language use relate to the cognitive abilities associated with language use in a school setting? If the child tests low on the former, how do educators ensure that he or she will achieve the latter? For exit purposes, "it is recommended that cognitively-demanding context-reduced measures be used because these more accurately reflect the communicative demands of an all English classroom". In the absence of a concrete example the question that immediately comes to mind is what exactly such a test would look like. There is the possibility that the exit tests prescribed by Cummins' model would resemble traditional IQ tests since it has been well established that such tests correlate highly with academic achievement and thereby have predictive validity. Use of exit tests that resemble IQ tests, however, may be undesirable for a number of reasons. Such a procedure would embroil bilingual educators in the emotional rancour and as yet unresolved psychometric problems that have surrounded the use of such tests with minority group children in the past (Loehlin, Lindzey & Spuhler, 1975). Intelligence-type tests are also less than desirable because they explain very little, albeit they have high predictive validity. Indeed, while the recommendation to use tests that are related to the communicative demands of an all English classroom for exit purposes makes good psychometric sense, it nevertheless brings up the question of why differences measured by the test occur in the first place. The claim that minority language children lack academic language skills in L2 because they lack them in L1 does little to answer this question.

Conclusion

It is agreed here that Cummins' introductory statement is a valid one:

> "... a major reason for the confused state of the art of languae proficiency assessment in bilingual programs (and indeed for the confusion surrounding the rationale for bilingual education) stems from the failure to develop an adequate theoretical framework for relating language proficiency to academic achievement."

It is not agreed, however, that such a framework is likely to emerge from a consideration of language alone without a serious and detailed understanding of the broader social context in which language development and use occur. It was pointed out, for example, that Cummins' conceptualization of language use in academic and non-academic settings artificially isolates language in academic settings from its social context and overemphasizes the nonsocial aspects of academic performance. It was also pointed out that language alone is not likely to explain the developmental lag that some minority language children experience in the acquisition of school-related language proficiency. This conclusion seems inescapable in view of the fact that some majority language children also experience this lag. Thus, the types of language proficiencies that Cummins postulates may best be conceived as intervening effects rather than as causal factors. Consequently, it may be premature to develop test programs, or even bilingual education curricula, on the basis of these putative language proficiencies without understanding their relationship with more fundamental causal factors. In the final analysis it is the underlying causal factors and their relationships to academic achievement that need to be uncovered. Cummins has made a valuable step in this direction, but it does not appear that the whole story is in yet.

References

Bruck, M. 1982, Language impaired children's performance in an additive bilingual education program. *Applied Psycholinguistics*, 3, 45–60.
Canale, M. & Swain, M. 1980, Theoretical bases of communicative approaches to second language teaching and testing. *Applied Linguistics*, 1(1), 1–47.
Cole, M. & Bruner, J. 1971, Cultural differences and inferences about psychological processes. *American Psychologist*, 26, 867–76.
Cole, M., Gay, J., Glick, J. A. & Sharp, D. W. 1971, *The cultural context of learning and thinking: An exploration in experimental anthropology*. New York: Basic Books.
Cummins, J. 1980, The entry and exit fallacy in bilingual education. *NABE Journal*, 4(3).
Genesee, F. 1981, A comparison of early and late second language learning. *Canadian Journal of Behavioural Sciences*, 13, 115–27.
Krashen, S., Long, M. & Scarcella, R. 1979, Age, rate and eventual attainment in second language acquisition. *TESOL Quarterly*, 13, 573–82.
Loehlin, J. C., Lindzey, G. & Spuhler, J. N. 1975, *Race differences in intelligence*. San Francisco: W. H. Freeman.
Nelson, K. 1981, Individual differences in language development: Implications for development and language. *Developmental Psychology*, 17(2), 170–87.
Vygotsky, L. S. 1962, *Thought and language*. Cambridge, Mass.: M.I.T. Press.

On some theoretical frameworks for language proficiency[1]

Michael Canale
The Ontario Institute for Studies in Education

The purpose of this chapter is to attempt to explain three widespread and nontrivial findings in recent work on language proficiency testing:

1. Certain individuals (often members of language minority groups) have been misclassified as having language disorders and "linguistic deficits", that is, as lacking in *basic language proficiency* (cf. Canale & Mougeon, 1978; Damico, Oller & Storey, 1981; Cummins, 1981, Hayes, 1983).
2. Certain students who have studied a second language in a formal classroom setting, and who perform well on academically-oriented second language tests, do not perform (as) well on tests requiring use of the second language for *authentic communication* outside such classroom settings (cf. Savignon, 1972; Tucker, 1974; and Upshur & Palmer, 1974).
3. Certain second language learners who perform well on tests requiring authentic communication in the second language may lack the language skills required to perform *academically-oriented autonomous tasks* — such as solving mathematical problems — presented in the second language (Cummins, in press; Cummins, 1981; Cummins, 1983).[2]

It is argued here that to account for such superficially diverse findings it is necessary to posit a theoretical framework that minimally distinguishes three dimensions of the notion "language proficiency"; basic, communicative, and autonomous proficiencies. As has been pointed out elsewhere, lack of an adequate theoretical framework remains the most fundamental problem in both language testing (cf. Palmer & Bachman, 1981; Cummins,

1983; Canale, 1983) and other domains of assessment (cf. Shoemaker, 1980 and references there).

This Chapter is organized into three sections: Section 1 critically reviews some recent work by Bruner and Cummins on various aspects of language proficiency; Section 2 outlines a theoretical framework that builds on this earlier work and responds to some of its inadequacies; and Section 3 provides some concluding remarks on the importance of such a framework for addressing other issues in language testing research such as validation procedures and interpretation of results.

Some recent frameworks for language proficiency

It is generally agreed that language proficiency is composed of underlying abilities, knowledge systems, and skills (e.g. Chomsky, 1980; Hymes, 1972; Oller, 1979). However, there is less agreement on the content and boundaries of this underlying competence and hence on what should be measured by language proficiency tests. As Cummins (this volume) observes, characterizations of language proficiency have ranged from a single (global) factor to 64 separate components. Clearly, there is no nonarbitrary upper limit on the number of components that could be theorized. However, it is assumed here that a more general characterization is both desirable (for reasons discussed in Popham, 1975, Chapter 7) and adequate to describe the core dimensions of language proficiency. Two general characterizations that seem specially instructive are those of Bruner (1975) and Cummins (1983; in press).

Bruner (1975) distinguishes three levels of language proficiency: linguistic competence, communicative competence, and analytic competence. The first two constitute, in his view, the "species minimum", where linguistic competence is used in its strong Chomskyan sense to refer to universals of grammar, and communicative competence refers to rules of social language use (e.g. appropriateness conditions as proposed by Grice, 1975). The third component, analytic competence, is concerned with the "context-free" use of language as an internal "technique of representation". In Bruner's own words:

"It involves the prolonged operation of thought processes exclusively on linguistic representations and propositional structures, accompanied by strategies of thought and problem-solving appropriate not to direct experience with objects and events but with ensembles of propositions. It is heavily metalinguistic in nature, in the sense of the use of this mode, involving operations on the linguistic code to assure its fit to sets of observations and it is strikingly the case that, more often than not, it generates new notational systems like mathematics, or more powerfully elaborated forms of the natural language like poetry" (1975, pp. 72–73).

An example may be helpful: Bruner cites the naming of the states in the United States in alphabetical order versus listing them in an order based on geographical considerations.

This theoretical framework is of interest for several reasons. For instance, it recognizes that a minimal characterization of language proficiency— Bruner's "species minimum"— includes both the language code and rules for use of this code in communicative contexts. This view is not always reflected in language proficiency tests, where often only mastery of the language code is addressed. Yet, growing evidence suggests that tests focussing on both form and use may provide more accurate assessment of both language proficiency (e.g. Farhady, 1980; Hayes, 1983) and language disorders (e.g. Damico, Oller & Storey, 1981). A second advantage of Bruner's framework is its recognition of an important use of language other than communication, namely, an analytic use for problem-solving and other intrapersonal tasks. Such recognition is especially welcome given the popular association of language use exclusively with communication in recent work on second language teaching and testing (cf. Canale & Swain, 1980; Cummins, in press, for discussion). Finally, the dimensions of language proficiency identified by Bruner bear on the three findings mentioned in the previous section.

However, this framework may be questioned on at least three grounds:

1. By excluding analytic competence from the "species minimum", Bruner gives the impression that such competence is not universal but only developed within certain individuals. Aside from permitting (even inviting) socially dangerous notions such as "cognitive deficits" and "racial superiority/inferiority", such an impression is quite gratuitous. Bruner presents no evidence nor reason that such competence should be excluded from the "species minimum" nor, for that matter, regarded as the highest form of language proficiency.
2. There is no clear distinction between the linguistic versus other cognitive demands made on the language user by a given communicative or analytic task. For example, a communicative task such as making an oral presentation on white-water canoeing

tactics might be more cognitively than linguistically demanding; whereas, a task such as conveying "sweet nothings" to one's lover may (as the term implies) be more linguistically than cognitively challenging. To draw conclusions about a person's language proficiency on the basis of an otherwise cognitively demanding task requires much care and caution.

3. One may question the dichotomous characterization of communication as context-dependent, tied to immediate external reality, and analytic language use as context-independent. For instance, in normal communication one frequently provides information that is in no clear way predictable — in form or content — from the immediate context nor bound to external reality: such information may deal with past, hypothetical, or false contexts and realities, for example, which can be created and imagined but not observed. As for analytic language use, it may be more context-independent with respect to immediate and observable reality but it is difficult to view any meaningful use of language as totally context-free. The context may be created and imaginary but it nonetheless exists, in some form, presumably in the mind of the mathematician, poet, or other analytic language user.

Cummins (1983; in press; 1981) has suggested a theoretical framework that responds to some of the inadequacies in Bruner's work and builds on its strong points. The framework described in this volume (Chapter 1) is a revision and clarification of an earlier model distinguishing basic interpersonal communicative skills from cognitive-academic language proficiency. It highlights the notions of contextual support and cognitive involvement, as schematized in Figure 1.

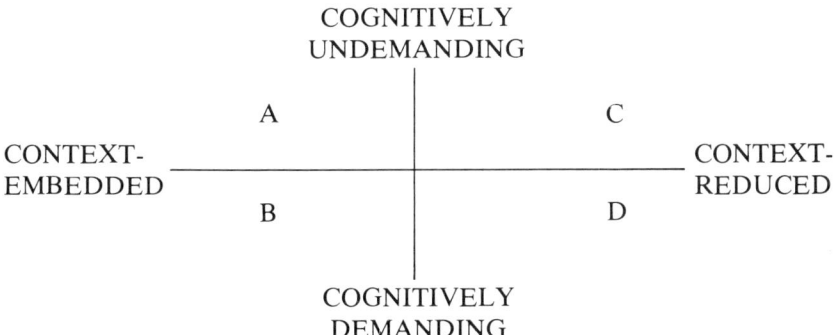

FIGURE 1 Cummins' Framework for Language Proficiency

The notion of contextual support and cognitive demand allow classification of language tasks into four primary groups, identified in Figure 1 by quadrants A through D. They do not necessarily represent increasing order of overall difficulty and developmental sequence. More context-embedded tasks (quadrants A and B) are characterized by Cummins as allowing active "negotiation of meaning" (e.g. requests for clarification and repetition), reliance on nonverbal and situational cues for transmitting and receiving information, and, more generally, support of a "shared reality" or common world knowledge. More context-reduced tasks (quadrants C and D) are claimed to require greater reliance on linguistic cues to meaning and on the propositional and logical structure of the information involved rather than on a shared (or even existing) reality. Cummins (1981) suggests the following tasks as examples at points along this continuum going from left to right: engaging in a discussion, writing a letter to a close friend, and writing (or reading) an academic article.

The vertical continuum groups together tasks that demand little active cognitive involvement or attention (quadrants A and C) as distinct from those involving much active processing of a large variety of information (quadrants B and D). As examples ranging from top to bottom on this axis one may cite pronunciation in one's dominant language, completing a routine homework assignment, and writing a major paper on a complex topic.

In addition to the compelling empirical and theoretical motivation cited by Cummins for this theoretical framework, it appears to be more satisfactory than Bruner's framework for addressing the concerns presented here. Thus, it not only has the advantages of Bruner's framework (e.g. focussing on more than just the language code and face-to-face interpersonal communication) but also responds to many of the inadequacies in Bruner's work suggested above. For example, it makes no claim that any one of the four types of task is beyond the "species minimum". Also, it recognizes a fundamental distinction between the linguistic and other cognitive demands involved in language use. Finally, it offers a nondichotomous characterization of interpersonal and intrapersonal language tasks by providing continua along which such tasks may range.

Although this is a potentially valuable framework for handling a variety of needs and findings involving language proficiency, it currently lacks sufficient clarity in at least four important respects.

First, there are questions about the classification of tasks according to this framework. For instance, Cummins equates "language proficiency" with "communicative proficiency" to emphasize the importance of the broader social context in which language proficiency develops. While such an equation may serve this purpose, it also gives the questionable impression that communication is the only or most important use of language. This is unfortunate since Cummins clearly recognizes other uses of language (e.g. problem-solving) and, just as clearly, their importance (cf. also Bruner, 1975; Chomsky, 1975; Chomsky, 1980; Jakobson, 1960). Another question of classification involves anomalous cases (i.e. where his framework makes either arbitrary or no predictions). For example, certain tasks may share both content-embedded and context-reduced features (e.g. allow "negotiation of meaning" and reliance on nonverbal and situational cues yet not deal with a shared reality and familiar or existing world knowledge): Are such tasks to be classified as more context-embedded or context-reduced?

This example introduces a second problem, that of the adequacy of the notion of contextual support as described by Cummins. What are the relevant features of context that must be present to facilitate expression and understanding of a message? How predictable are the form and content of a message except in very routine and formulaic language use? How do contextual cues differ in spoken and written uses of language and how important are these differences? How fixed and definable is context (again except in routine and formulaic language use — cf. Haley, 1963)? Until such questions are more clearly addressed, more adequate criteria than contextual support may consist of ones such as degree of social and cultural exposure to various language tasks (familiarity) and acceptance of them (cf. Cook-Gumperz & Gumperz, 1981; Tannen, 1980; Genesee, this volume; Troike, this volume).

A third issue involves the order of difficulty and developmental sequence regarding the four general types of tasks (A through D) in Figure 1. While it seems clear that tasks of types A and D represent the extremes concerning difficulty and developmental sequence, it is not clear how tasks of types B and C are ordered with respect to one another. On the one hand, it might be argued that since tasks of type C are less cognitively demanding than those of type B, the former are ordered before the latter (by definition). On the other hand, Cummins recognizes that contextual support can facilitate performance and mastery of otherwise cognitively demanding tasks, suggesting that type B tasks might be ordered before type C ones.

Finally, and perhaps most seriously, it is not clear how Cummins's framework handles two of the three sets of findings referred to in the introductory section above. This framework seems quite adequate (and was specifically designed) to handle the finding that performance on authentic communication takes in a second language is not always a good predictor of performance on academically-oriented autonomous tasks presented in the second language. However, it fails to provide an adequate notion of basic language proficiency to explain why certain individuals are (accidentally) misclassified as having language disorders and "linguistic deficits", and it fails to explain why some students who perform well on academically-oriented autonomous tasks — which, presumably would be classified as C and D tasks in this framework — do not perform as well on authentic communication tasks — presumably tasks of types A and B (see Tucker, 1974, for examples).

A suggested theoretical framework

In order to address such findings more adequately and to respond to some of the other shortcomings of previous frameworks for language proficiency, it is suggested here that a theoretical framework with the following three general features is needed: (a) basic, communicative, and autonomous language proficiencies must be distinguished; (b) the types of knowledge and skill involved in each of these language proficiency areas must be identified; and (c) the linguistic and other cognitive demands must be considered separately for a given language task. Thus, for each of the three dimensions of language proficiency under (a), it is proposed that one must specify the prerequisite language-related competencies as well as the contributions of both linguistic and nonlinguistic demands to the difficulty of the task in question. The remainder of this section first proposes a preliminary range of language-related competence areas and then sketches the general properties of the three proficiency dimensions.

As a preliminary range of language knowledge and skill areas, one might consider the general framework proposed by Canale & Swain (1980) based on earlier work by Hymes (1972) and Morrow (1977), among others. Although proposed originally for only communicative language use, this framework may be useful for understanding other uses of language as well. Its main components are presented in Canale (1983) as follows:

1. *Grammatical competence*: mastery of the language code (e.g. lexical items and rules of word formation, sentence formation, literal meaning, pronunciation, and spelling).
2. *Sociolinguistic competence*: mastery of appropriate use and understanding of language in different sociolinguistic contexts, with emphasis on appropriateness of both meanings (e.g. topics, functions) and forms (e.g. register, formulaic expressions).
3. *Discourse competence*: mastery of how to combine and interpret meanings and forms to achieve unified text in different genres (e.g.

casual conversation, argumentative essay, or recipe) by using (a) cohesion devices to relate forms (e.g. use of pronouns, synonyms, transition words, and parallel structures) and (b) coherence rules to organize meanings (e.g. concerning the selection, sequencing, consistency, and balance of ideas).

4. *Strategic competence*: mastery of verbal and nonverbal strategies both (a) to compensate for breakdowns in communication due to insufficient competence or to performance limitations (e.g. use of paraphrase) and (b) to enhance the rhetorical effect of utterances (e.g. use of slow, soft speech). (For further discussion of these competence areas, see Canale & Swain, 1980; Canale, 1983).

With this range of competencies in mind, consider the three dimensions of language proficiency: basic, communicative, and autonomous proficiencies.

1. *Basic language proficiency.*
This dimension is concerned with the biological universals required for any language development and use. Of concern, then, are not only universals of grammar that underlie grammatical competence (e.g. Chomsky, 1975, 1980) but also sociolinguistic universals (e.g. Grice, 1975), discourse universals (e.g. Charolles, 1978), strategic universals (e.g. Bialystok, 1979; Tarone, 1981), and perceptual processing universals (e.g. Bever, 1970). It is assumed that such universals interact with general cognitive development to determine possible uses, messages, and forms of language. The potential value of such an enriched notion of basic language proficiency is suggested in the work of Damico, Oller and Storey (1981), for example, where their focus in diagnosis of language disorders includes not only a wide variety of aspects of language use but also more universal versus superficial, language-specific features.

2. *Communicative language proficiency.*
The focus here is on social, interpersonal uses of language through spoken or written channels. It is assumed with Morrow (1977) and others that communication is primarily a form of social interaction in which emphasis is normally placed less on grammatical forms and literal meaning than on participants and their purposes in using language (i.e. on the social meaning of utterances). Such social meaning is qualified by contextual variables such as role of participants, setting, purposes, and norms of interaction. Authentic communication thus requires continuous evaluation and negotiation of various levels of information (cf. Candlin, 1981; Haley, 1963; Hymes, 1972). Such contextual variables may serve to simplify communication (i.e. by providing clues to meaning) or complicate it (e.g. by

imposing language-specific appropriateness conditions). Although communication normally involves grammatical, sociolinguistic, discourse, and strategic competences (as identified above), the focus in this use of language may be primarily on sociolinguistic and strategic knowledge and skills. As such, the degree of exposure to and use of sociolinguistic rules and communication strategies — that is, degree of socialization and acculturation with respect to a particular language community — may be especially important in determining the range of communicative functions and situations that an individual can and is willing to handle.

3. *Autonomous language proficiency.*
This dimension involves proficiency in less directly social, more intrapersonal uses of language such as problem solving, monitoring one's thoughts, verbal play, poetry and creative writing. Focus is less on social meaning than on grammatical forms, organization of ideas, and literal meaning. Hence, contextual variables do not serve to qualify (simplify or complicate) information as much as do the language code and logical relationships among propositions. Though immediate sociolinguistic context may be rich, it is not necessarily in focus in autonomous language uses (for example, counting one's change at the local grocery store). The main language competences involved would seem to be grammatical (especially vocabulary and rules of sentence formation and literal meaning) and discourse, with less contribution of strategic competence and the least demand on sociolinguistic competence. Again, degree of socialization (e.g. degree of exposure to and acceptance of various autonomous tasks in a given language) may be viewed as a valuable index of the range of such tasks that can be performed by an individual through that same language without undue affective, linguistic and general cognitive difficulties.

To summarize, the relationships among these three dimensions of language proficiency seem to be as follows. Basic language proficiency is comprised of those language-related universals that are required for communicative and autonomous language uses. However, such universals constitute only the biological upper limits — and, hence, only a part — of these other dimensions; the remainder of an individual's communicative and autonomous proficiency is presumably the result of socialization and, to some extent, individual differences in personality, intelligence, learning style, motivation, and personal experiences. Communicative and autonomous proficiencies seem to differ in that sociolinguistic and strategic competencies receive emphasis in communicative language uses whereas grammatical and discourse competencies may be more in focus in autonomous uses.[3] On this view it follows that one cannot adequately develop or test communicative proficiency through autonomous tasks nor vice versa.

Concluding Remarks

The theoretical framework outlined in the preceding section lacks sufficient detail to qualify as anything more than a working hypothesis on the contents and boundaries of language proficiency. Nonetheless, it is proposed as a more adequate hypothesis than others considered here for handling the three sets of findings presented in the introductory section.

In addition to its relevance to such findings, the proposed framework may have some interesting implications in two other areas of language testing: validation procedures and interpretation of results.

With respect to validation procedures, this framework addresses important concerns in the domains of construct, content, and criterion-referenced (concurrent and predictive) validity. Thus in the domain of construct validity, not only has a theoretical construct for language proficiency been proposed and tentatively examined, but the types of test methods (tasks) suitable for assessing different dimensions of language proficiency have also been suggested. This compatibility of objective (or trait) and assessment method has been identified by Palmer & Bachman (1981) and others as a fundamental concern in construct validation. As for content validity, this framework offers some indication — albeit very general and speculative — of the proportion, relative difficulty, and interrelationships of the various knowledge and skill areas involved in each dimension of language proficiency. Finally, as concerns criterion-referenced validity, this framework suggests that care must be taken in identifying criterion groups (e.g. who may not necessarily share the same degree of socialization as the test group), criterion instruments (e.g. which may be more communication- than autonomous-oriented), and predicted outcomes (e.g. which may be questioned since communicative and autonomous proficiencies may presumably change — that is, increase or decrease — over relatively short periods of time due to changes in degree of exposure to and use of a given language for given tasks).

With respect to interpretation of results, the proposed framework has two important implications. First, one must not confuse linguistic demands with other cognitive demands made by a given task: To do so may contribute to incorrect conclusions about the language proficiency and even general cognitive proficiency of individuals (e.g. in the form of labels such as "linguistic deficit" and "cognitive deficit"). Second, this framework stresses the potential contribution of socialization and acculturation to performance on a given language task. Performance on language proficiency tests may be influenced by individuals' attitudes toward and acceptance of certain tasks (cf. Cook-Gumperz & Gumperz, 1981; Tannen, 1980; Shohamy, 1980) as well as by dialect differences (cf. Canale & Mougeon, 1978), for example. As Troike (this volume) points out, "all testing is a social (and usually sociolinguistic) event, constituted and constructed by the participants in the event". In this light, test results may be better viewed as *created* rather than simply observed or found.

As the focus in language proficiency testing shifts from knowledge of grammatical forms to a variety of uses of language, it is crucial that previous theoretical frameworks for language proficiency be reassessed and new possibilities explored. At the same time, it is important to keep in mind that language proficiency is only one of many complex and little understood cognitive systems that interact in performance of any language task. Research on language proficiency is crucial to the field of language testing but it is only part of a broader, multidisciplinary effort. In a similar vein, language proficiency itself, although related to academic achievement, can only serve as one among many perhaps more important variables for predicting and influencing a child's chances of succeeding in an academic environment.

Notes

1. This is a slightly revised version of a chapter entitled "On some dimensions of language proficiency", which appears in J. W. Oller, Jr. (ed.), 1983, *Issues in language testing research*, Newbury House.
2. I would like to thank Jim Cummins and Ellen Rosansky for helpful discussion of the views expressed here. I assume full responsibility for all content errors, of course.
3. See Bachman and Palmer (1983) for discussion of findings that support the grouping proposed here of grammatical and discourse competencies on the one hand, and sociolinguistic and strategic competencies on the other.

References

Bachman, L. & Palmer, A. S. 1983, The construct validation of some components of communicative proficiency. In C. Rivera (ed.) *Communicative Competence Approaches to Language Proficiency Assessment: Research and Application.* Clevedon, England: Multilingual Matters.

Bever, T. G. 1970, The cognitive basis for linguistic structures. In J. R. Hayes (ed.), *Cognition and the development of language*. New York: John Wiley and Sons.

Bialystok, E. 1979, The role of conscious strategies in second language proficiency. *Canadian Modern Language Review*, 35, 372–94.

Bruner, J. S. 1975, Language as an instrument of thought. In A. Davies (ed.), *Seminar on language and learning: Problems of language and learning.* London: Heinemann.
Canale, M. 1983, A communicative approach to language proficiency assessment in a minority setting. In C. Rivera (ed.) *Communicative Competence Approaches to Language Proficiency Assessment: Research and Application.* Clevedon, England: Multilingual Matters.
— 1983, From communicative competence to communicative language pedagogy. In J. C. Richards and R. Schmidt (eds), *Language and communication*. Book in preparation.
Canale, M. & Mougeon, R. 1978, Problèmes posés par la mesure du rendement en français des élèves franco-ontariens. In *Working Papers on Bilingualism*, 16, 92–110.
Canale, M. & Swain, M. 1980, Theoretical bases of communicative approaches to second language teaching and testing. *Applied Linguistics*, 1(1), 1–47.
Candlin, C. N. 1981, Discoursal patterning and the equalising of interpretive opportunity. In L. Smith (ed.), *English for cross-cultural communication*. New York: St. Martin's Press.
Charolles, M. 1978, Introduction aux problèmes de la cohérence des textes. *Langue française*, 38, 7–41.
Chomsky, N. 1975, *Reflections on language*, New York: Pantheon Books.
— 1980, *Rules and representations*. New York: Columbia University Press.
Cook-Gumperz, J. & Gumperz, J. J. 1981, From oral to written culture: The transition to literacy. In M. F. Whiteman (ed.), *Variation in writing*. New York: Lawrence Erlbaum.
Cummins, J. 1981, *The role of primary language development in promoting educational success for language minority students*. In the California State Department of Education (ed.), *Compendium on bilingual-bicultural education*.
— in press, Is academic achievement distinguishable from language proficiency? In J. W. Oller, Jr. (ed.), *Current issues in language testing research*. Rowley, Mass.: Newbury House.
Damico, J., Oller, J. W. & Storey, M. E. 1981, The diagnosis of language disorders in bilingual children: Pragmatic and surface-oriented criteria. In J. Erickson & D. Omark (eds), *The bilingual exceptional child*. Springfield, Ill.: Charles C. Thomas.
Farhady, H. 1980, *Justification, development, and validation of functional language tests*. Unpublished doctoral dissertation, University of California at Los Angeles.
Grice, H. P. 1975, Logic and conversation. In P. Cole & J. J. Morgan (eds), *Syntax and semantics: Speech acts* (Vol. 3). New York: Academic Press.
Haley, J. 1963, *Strategies of psychotherapy*. New York: Grune and Stratton.
Hayes, Z. A. 1983, *"Limited" language proficiency of Mexican-American 3rd Grade students: A problem in the definition and measurement of bilingualism*. In C. Rivera (ed.), *Communicative Competence Approaches to Language Proficiency Assessment: Research and Application*, Clevedon, England: Multilingual Matters.
Hymes, D. 1972, On communicative competence. In J. B. Pride & J. Holmes (eds), *Sociolinguistics*. Harmondsworth, England: Penguin Books.
Jakobson, R. 1960, Concluding statement: Linguistics and poetics. In T. A. Sebeok (ed.), *Style in language*. Cambridge, Mass.: MIT Press.

Morrow, K. 1977, *Techniques of evaluation for a notional syllabus*. London: The Royal Society of Arts.
Oller, Jr., J. W. 1979, *Language tests at school*. London: Longman.
Palmer, A. S., & Bachman, L. 1981, Basic concerns in test validation. In J. Read (ed.), *Proceedings of the Regional Language Center (RELC) Seminar on Evaluation and Measurement of Language Competence and Performance*. Singapore: Regional Language Center.
Popham, W. J. 1975, *Educational evaluation*. Englewood Cliffs, N. J.: Prentice-Hall.
Savignon, S. J. 1972, *Communicative competence: An experiment in foreign-language teaching*. Philadelphia: Center for Curriculum Development.
Shoemaker, D. M. 1980, Improving achievement testing. *Educational Evaluation and Policy Analysis*, 2(6), 37–49.
Shohamy, E. 1980, *Students' attitudes toward tests: Affective considerations in language testing*. Paper presented at the TESOL '80 Meeting, San Francisco, March, Mimeo.
Tannen, D. 1980, Implications of the oral/literate continuum for cross-cultural communication. In J. E. Alatis (ed.), *Georgetown University Round Table on Languages and Linguistics, 1980*. Washington, D.C.: Georgetown University Press.
Tarone, E. 1981, Some thoughts on the notion of communication strategy. *TESOL Quarterly*, 15(3), 285–95.
Tucker, G. R. 1974, The assessment of bilingual and bicultural factors of communication. In S. T. Carey (ed.), *Bilingualism, biculturalism, and education*. Edmonton: University of Alberta Press.
Upshur, J. A. & Palmer, A. S. 1974, Measures of accuracy, communicativity, and social judgements for two classes of foreign language speakers. In A. Verdoodt (ed.), *3rd International Congress of Applied Linguistics: Copenhagen, 1972: Applied sociolinguistics* (Vol. 2). Heidelberg: Julius Groos Verlag.

A note on the dangers of terminological innovation

Bernard Spolsky
Bar-Ilan University

In astronomy and zoology, there are strict rules and formal procedures for the naming of new stars and new species. In the human and social sciences, we are much less rigorous about terminological innovation, but we should still, I believe, object to particularly egregious examples of misleading labelling. Such a case happened when Cummins (1979) coined the terms Basic Interpersonal Communicative Skills and Cognitive Academic Language Proficiency, and the problem was compounded when he and some of his colleagues started to use acronyms (BICS and CALP) for these new labels.

I realize that my dislike for acronyms may be idiosyncratic, but I nonetheless believe that rather than becoming more precise, acronyms encourage greater vagueness. For example, by constantly using the abbreviations L1 and L2, we are able to avoid explaining (or being sure) exactly what we mean by a first or second language: if we used the full expression, we would be more likely to remember to make clear whether we refer to the language first learned, or the language most used in the home, or the mother's language, or the stronger language, or any of the other possibly relevant dimensions. We might, of course, want to refer to all of these possible meanings, but the transparent term will help remind us of the need for definition.

One of the problems with Cummins' terms is in the value judgements they carry with them. "Proficiency" may not seem very much better than "skills", but "cognitive" and "academic" are surely more valued than "basic". More serious is the confusion of dimensions that goes along with the labelling; what Cummins has chosen to do is to explain the clustering of two kinds of tests as evidence of different underlying clusters of abilities. There are other interpretations, and I want to suggest one later.

We are concerned here with characterizing the way people use language, and of measuring their underlying knowledge. Here, too, we have terminological problems, brought on in large measure by Chomsky's infelicitous use of the term "linguistic competence" (1965) to refer to the abstract set of rules expressing the syntax of a language, and the counter-proposal by Hymes (1972) to use the term 'communicative competence" to refer to the rules governing all aspects of systematic language use. Both of these go against a normal language use of the term "competence" to mean ability. Seeing that we expect to be able to measure what in normal language we call competence, we expect to be able to measure Chomskyan or Hymesian competence, but the former definitely and the latter probably are, by definition, too abstract to measure. But this is what we must expect of a field that persists in using a term for itself that is regularly misunderstood by laymen. (How often will linguists need to deny that they are polyglots before they are ready to change the name of their field?)

Whatever we call the ability to use language, it is clear that it is very complex, not unitary, and measurable along a number of different dimensions. You might measure how well my pronunciation compares to a native speaker's, or how clear it is over a telephone; you might count the number of different words I use in a talk, or the speed of my syllable production; you might observe the structure of my sentences, or the effectiveness of my speech acts. Each of these measurements is likely to be different, and each of these dimensions is likely to be of different relevance to different social situations.

Put another way, it seems that the minimal level of language ability on a particular dimension is just as socially determined as other minimal levels of social ability. Communities and situations set different requirements for performance. For instance, while I expect a foreign student in a second language class to make a major effort to pronounce everything carefully, I am prepared to make a great effort to understand the strange accent of a visiting scholar whose work is important to me.

I believe this flexibility is part of the explanation of Cummin's observations. In various kinds of interpersonal communication, there are different minimal levels of performance expected. The factor of interlocutor tolerance or co-operation, most clearly exemplified by such special cases as baby talk, foreigner talk, and teacher talk, is a critical element in face-to-face communication. There is, in fact, a broad scale of communicative ability: We know how to refer to the high level of interpersonal communicative skills of a good salesman or a fine political speaker, but the minimal levels, as tested by those tests Cummins labelled basic, are in fact much lower, involving as they do situations of maximal interlocutor co-operation.

But there is one situation where co-operation and tolerance are minimized, an area where there is a rigid insistence on particular kinds of language, and this is the variety of academic language chosen as its ideal by the Western literate tradition. The style is one that favors autonomous verbalization, that idealizes the communication to relative strangers of the maximum amount of new knowledge using only verbal means. This style idealized within our educational tradition, is not favored by other cultures, or by other educational systems. It is however the method of communication that is most likely to be tapped by formal language tests, which are themselves by definition the least tolerant and co-operative of any communication situation.

In Cummins' original formulation, his contrast between these sets of tests fell into the same trap as Bernstein did: a useful observation of the existence of different styles was vitiated by a readiness to apply labels, and these labels set up a false dichotomy that was itself socially dangerous. I am gratified by Cummins' willingness to stop using the old terms, and am sure that this new openness will permit us to learn a great deal from his observations.

References

Chomsky, N. 1965, *Aspects of the theory of syntax*. Cambridge: MIT Press.
Cummins, J. 1979, Linguistic interdependence and the educational development of bilingual children. *Review of Educational Research*, 49(2), 225–51.
— 1980a, The cross-lingual dimensions of language proficiency: Implications for bilingual education and the optimal age issue. *TESOL Quarterly*, 14(2), 175–88.
— 1980b Psychological assessment of immigrant children: Logic or intuition? *Journal of Multilingual and Multicultural Development*, 1(2), 97–111.
— 1980c The construct of language proficiency in bilingual education. In J. Alatis (ed.), *Georgetown University Round Table on Languages and Linguistics 1980: Current issues in bilingual education*. Washington, D.C.: Georgetown University Press.
Hymes, D. 1972, On communicative competence. In J. B. Pride & J. Holmes (eds), *Sociolinguistics*. Harmondsworth, England: Penguin Books.

SCALP: Social and cultural aspects of language proficiency[1]

Rudolph C. Troike
Department of Educational Policy Studies,
University of Illinois at Urbana-Champaign

In a series of important papers in the past several years, James Cummins has proposed two major constructs as part of an effort to account for the phenomenon of low scholastic achievement commonly found among minority language children. Specifically, he has proposed (1979, 1980a) the existence of:

a) a "*cognitive/academic language proficiency*" (CALP), differing from other aspects of language proficiency, which forms the basis for academic development; and
b) a *threshold level* of proficiency in a first language (L1) which interacts with development of proficiency in a second language (L2).

The threshold concept was previously introduced by Skutnabb-Kangas & Toukomaa (1976) in their study of Finnish immigrant children in Sweden. Cummins (1979) has integrated the CALP and threshold concepts in what he has called the "linguistic interdependence hypothesis", viz that the level of second language (L2) competence which a bilingual child attains is partially a function of the type of competence the child has developed in the first language (L1) at the time when intensive exposure to L2 begins (p. 233). An earlier formulation of this hypothesis was expressed by Toukomaa & Skutnabb-Kangas (1977) as follows: "The basis for the possible attainment of the threshold level of L2 competence seems to be the level attained in the mother tongue" (p. 28).

The Finnish researchers and Cummins (1979) have suggested that *lower* and *higher thresholds* of proficiency should be recognized, with the lower threshold being minimally adequate for nonacademic purposes, and the higher threshold being a precondition for academic success. The lower threshold would presumably have some similarity to what Cummins (1980a) has since called "basic interpersonal communication skills" (BICS). Cummins and Swain (1980), as well as Lambert, Tucker, and others have been at great pains to distinguish the circumstances surrounding the successful achievement of middle-class English speaking students in French "immersion" programs in Canada from the more common situation of "submersion" of linguistic minority children in national-language-medium school programs. Cummins advances his "linguistic interdependence hypothesis" to explain the apparently contradictory findings that students in immersion programs satisfactorily learn the L2 and suffer no loss in their native language proficiency, while minority students in submersion programs frequently lose proficiency in their native language and at the same time fail to attain adequate proficiency in the school language, conditions Lambert (1975) has labelled "additive bilingualism" and "subtractive bilingualism" respectively.

At issue here will be several questions:

1. Is CALP a valid construct?
2. How do individual, social, and interactional factors bear on the interdependence hypothesis?
3. What is the significance of social and contextual factors in the development and assessment of language proficiency and academic achievement?
4. How do cultural factors affect academic achievement?

In one of Cummins' (1980b) most recent papers, he indicates that:

"with the exception of severely retarded and autistic children, everybody acquires basic interpersonal communicative skills (BICS) in a first language, regardless of IQ or academic aptitude" (p. 84).

He then adopts the "iceberg" metaphor to portray BICS as "surface-level" (manifestational) proficiency, while CALP is "deep level" (manipulative) ability. Bilingual competence is illustrated by a "dual iceberg model" (p. 87).

A minor caveat should be voiced in passing regarding the claim that "everybody acquires basic interpersonal communicative skills (BICS) in a first language". Hymes and others have pointed out that different language skills are differentially distributed in any community, and unless BICS is defined at an absolutely minimal level, there will be great variations in the extent to which individuals will be found to have mastered interpersonal communicative skills. To deny that would be to deny personality differences and most of psychology along with them, as well as individual differences in all social interaction skills.

With regard to CALP, probably it would first of all appear to a large extent to be identified closely with Oller's (1980a) general language proficiency factor. (Parenthetically, let me add that since in many respects this resembles Spearman's (1927) g factor of intelligence, we may term it Oller's glp.) Oller shows that in two separate studies, quite diverse language skills test subscores intercorrelate quite closely and that an average of three-fourths of the variance in each test is attributable to a single general factor. It can be suggested here that this factor, if it exists, is equivalent to CALP and to Spearman's g, and is based on the frequently reported correlation between language ability and intelligence (Cummins, 1980b; Vellutino, 1977, 1979; Carroll, 1979). Oller (1980b) has in fact explicitly equated his glp and Spearman's g.

While all of this, if true, is very exciting, it is also subject to question on sociolinguistic grounds as to whether a procedural artifact or a pseudo-phenomenon is involved here. It has been suggested that language tests and intelligence tests are tapping the same factor. If this factor is itself language ability rather than a hypothesized meta-ability, then the whole suggestion reduces to a vacuous tautology.

There are good reasons for suggesting why this may be so. Labov (1969) amply demonstrated the distorting sociolinguistic effects of a Bereiter and Engelmann-type interrogation of a Black child compared to an informal interview conducted in comfortable surroundings by a researcher of the same ethnic background. As is increasingly coming to be recognized, all testing is a social (and usually sociolinguistic; e.g. Upshur, 1973) event, constituted and constructed by the participants in the event. The extent to which this is reflected in test outcomes was shown several years ago in a study which found that when White and Black students were given a test by a human administrator versus by means of a computer, the White students' scores differed only marginally, while Black students' scores improved by one-third.

An even graver question arises with respect to the effect of reading ability on test scores. In general, it is assumed that reading ability measures will produce generally reliable results and that the ability tapped by the measures will show reasonable stability. However, various reading subskills have been shown to be subject to improvement by training, and even SAT scores have been raised through training. Furthermore, just changing motivation/incentive structures can produce improved reading achievement scores, as the *Reading Is Fundamental* (RIF) program has amply demonstrated. Merely by allowing children to choose books they wish to read and enabling them to buy them for a token price, their amount of reading and reading scores have increased, sometimes remarkably. A similar finding is reported from Austria (Bamberger, 1973).

Some of the training found to improve reading is admittedly largely linguistic in nature (e.g. the reading scores of a group of American Indian students rose after they were given lessons on vocabulary), and there is a well-known correlation between size of vocabulary and reading ability. However, reading researchers are increasingly coming to the realization that reading comprehension is highly affected by what they term "knowledge of the world".[2] Since this often correlates with socio-economic status (SES), reading achievement scores and school achievement generally are not surprisingly closely linked in many situations to SES, so much so that Karl Deutsch is reputed to have once said, "Tell me the father's income and I'll tell you the student's grades in school." The problematical work of Basil Bernstein (1975) also immediately comes to mind, showing linkages between discursive styles and social class, and raising questions regarding the possible causative connection between these styles and school achievement. Since this area of interpersonal sociolinguistic styles belongs by definition to BICS rather than to CALP, Cummins' formulation would presumably discount any explanatory nexus here.

The interrelationships among these factors cannot be easily dismissed, however. If SES or other socio-cultural factors (SCF) affect opportunities to gain "knowledge of the world" and sociolinguistic style, which in turn affect reading comprehension, then school achievement will certainly be affected (positively or negatively). This may be schematized as follows:

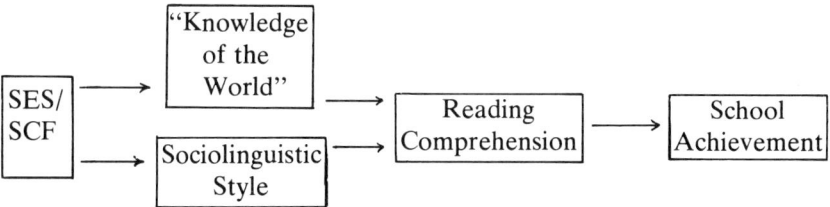

Further, some of these same factors affect intelligence measures:

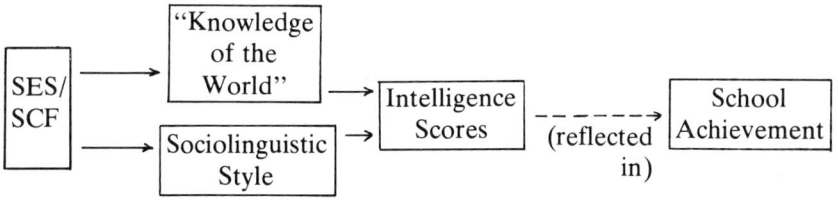

The effects of sociolinguistic style may be realized in part through the social environment created by the linguistic interaction between examiner and examinee, or the interaction between the examinee and the language of the examination. All of this would suggest that reading comprehension scores and intelligence scores are not independent, but reflect in one way or another some of the same input factors.

One must also be conscious of the widely studied but often difficult-to-assess effects of the mutually interacting social (and sometimes linguistically mediated) attitudes of students and teachers. The well known "Pygmalion effect" (Rosenthal & Jakobson, 1968) clearly has powerful consequences for lower SES and minority children. Teachers' expectations regarding student achievement become translated into self-fulfilling prophecies through differential treatment of students and perceptions of student performance. Negative teacher attitudes and behaviors toward the speech of such children also undoubtedly affect student performance: This was the rationale behind the recent Ann Arbor, Michigan, court decision which required teachers to take an in-service course in sociolinguistics.

The other side of the coin has to do with student attitudes. Strong affective ties serve to perpetuate nonstandard language in many societies, as shown by Willis' (1977) study in England and Rickford's (1980) in Guyana. At the same time, these positive peer group attitudes come to be buttressed by negative attitudes towards the language and culture of the school, and a rejection of the middle-class values and academic goal orientation represented and rewarded by the teacher and the school. Contrary survival skills are cultivated (see Abrahams & Gay, 1972; Willis, 1977) and rewarded in the peer group, producing a true lower SES or minority group counter-culture in the schools (sometimes extending to the formation of gangs and the development of gang warfare). While the leaders of such groups often display considerable intelligence, their interests and energies are channelled into ways that reject the reward structure of the school, and that presumably lead to a lowered CALP.

These observations lead further to a consideration of the content and function of schooling itself, at least as practiced in the Anglo-American tradition. It is clear that most modern education is class-based and class-oriented, and seeks to perpetuate middle-class values and culture, and to recruit and assimilate the lower classes and minorities into the middle class, or at least to co-opt them into accepting the legitimate domination of the middle class. Not surprisingly, one consequence of what Cárdenas and Cárdenas have called the "incompatibilities" of school culture and lower-class/minority culture (including language), is that the school has been accused by radical critics of simply reproducing social structure

(Bowles & Gintis, 1976), a situation summed up colloquially in the traditional motto, "Them as has, gits."

Viewed in a slightly different perspective, the situation is essentially what has been referred to as "internal colonialism". The term is somewhat metaphorical when applied to class domination, but in the case of conquered or otherwise subordinated ethnic/linguistic minorities, it takes on a quite literal meaning. Educated middle-class (tautologically, "standard") English is the instrument of this colonialism, in which linguistic and racial boundaries often coincide.

If school achievement, intelligence scores, and CALP all agree to a remarkable extent, might it not be that what they are reflecting is not some general underlying ability, but simply degree of acculturation to a culture-specific set of norms, the culture being that of the dominant middle class as reflected in the school?

CALP, then, and "intelligence" (for which CALP may be a surrogate or an equivalent construct) may be simply INDICATORS OF ACCULTURATION rather than of an independent mental ability.

The Skutnabb-Kangas and Toukomaa/Cummins linguistic interdependence hypothesis is a very attractive one, and has a certain amount of research evidence supporting it, notably that on Finnish immigrants in Sweden, and some on Mexican immigrants in the U.S. (Kimball, 1968). However, there is strong counterevidence, albeit of an inferential sort, which raises serious questions regarding the validity of the hypothesis. As I have pointed out elsewhere (Troike, 1978, 1981) the counterevidence suggests that social and cultural factors may be much more powerful than purely linguistic factors in influencing educational achievement, and, indeed, that the linguistic factors may be simply a second or third order reflection of the social and cultural context of schooling.

On the issue of the "threshold" relations of L1 and L2 proficiency, Dillon Platero (1981) recently reported on the case of two Navajo students, one of whom possessed limited proficiency in Navajo but graduated from the University of New Mexico with honors and went on to Stanford to study graduate physics, while the other had such remarkable proficiency in Navajo that he astounded his elders but barely made it through the University even with tutorial assistance because of his weakness in English.

The Finnish data have been very persuasive to a number of researchers, but there is anecdotal evidence from Australia to suggest that the effects are confounded with social factors. Finnish immigrants in Sweden are viewed very negatively by Swedes, and a number of negative stereotypes exist (it must be remembered that Finland was formerly a "colonial" possession of Sweden). In Australia, however, Finns are viewed in terms of a number of positive ("Scandinavian") stereotypes, and Finnish students do much better in school than do their counterparts in Sweden (Ilpola, 1979), once again demonstrating the Pygmalion effect.

Perhaps the most serious question regarding the linguistic interdependence hypothesis comes from school data in the U.S. Southwest and West which shows that in districts with Black, Hispanic, and Anglo children, there is a clear stratification of school achievement scores which places Blacks at the bottom, Anglos at the top, and Hispanics in between. Unless one wishes to adopt a Jensen-type genetic explanation, which I would strongly reject, the stratification can be interpreted as reflecting the existing social status of the three groups. However, since Blacks are native English speakers (albeit of a very distinctive variety) and most of the Hispanics involved have been "submerged" in English-medium education under classic conditions productive of subtractive bilingualism and semilingualism, nothing in the situation would lead to the prediction that Hispanics would score above Blacks in school achievement. It would certainly appear difficult to implicate language proficiency, particularly of the sort envisioned in CALP, as an explanatory factor, short of invoking genetics.

Language and culture may actually play an important role in determining such outcomes, though more in BICS-like ways than CALPish ones (ironically, the explanatory properties attributed to CALP might more appropriately attach to BICS). As suggested earlier, teacher (as well as community) attitudes toward a particular group may, via the Pygmalion effect, serve to raise or depress academic achievement. The home background effect has been ignored up to this point, other than the gross differentiation of SES by income levels. However, academic outcomes are always the complex results of interactions between the personal characteristics of the individual and his or her home/cultural background, and the physical, social, cultural, and human characteristics of the educational setting.

The interactive effects of home cultural background and school was shown in a study by Mace (1972) of the academic achievement of Hispanic, Filipino, and Chinese children in Seattle. Although all were at a comparably low income level, and had comparable entering knowledge of English at the first grade, by the third grade, Chinese children were well ahead of the others, and Filipinos were slightly ahead of Hispanic children. The traditional strong emphasis on academic achievement of Chinese families was probably an influencing factor, and no doubt this interacted with teacher expectations (and consequent behaviors) that Chinese children "always do well'.

To summarize, it has been demonstrated that reading and text-processing skills play a major role in determining school achievement, and that the development of these skills is affected in little-understood ways by home background, including SES, but may be interactionally stimulated or retarded both by pedagogical practices and by sociolinguistic/cultural attitudes, expectations, and behaviors manifested by the teacher and others (including peers and school administrators) in the school setting. The extent to which individual personality factors may be involved has only begun to be recognized (Wong-Fillmore, 1976; Edelsky & Hudelson, 1979, 1980), but the contribution of native endowment still remains to be isolated and identified.

I have suggested that sociolinguistic factors may play a much more important role than the "tip of the iceberg" status accorded them in Cummins' formulation. In addition, the general (language-mediated) cognitive-intellectual ability (Oller's glp) which he posits may be largely an artifact of test results that actually reflect acculturative approximations to middle-class Western cultural norms and behaviors. If we are to avoid reifying tautologies, we must be cautious about prematurely moving to draw conclusions or formulate models on the basis of inadequate and incompletely understood data. As Hamlet said to Horatio, "There are more things in heaven and earth than are dreamt of in your philosophies." We would do well to remember this precaution as we seek to understand the complex forces that shape children's cognitive and linguistic abilities.

Notes

1. If perceptive readers note a gentle spoof of Cummins' CALP in this title, it is their phenomenological right to such an interpretation, though I apologize in advance for it. I should like to note at the outset, that I am very sympathetic with one implication (or motivation) which I read into Cummins' proposal, viz that minority language children should be provided the opportunity to develop proficiency in their native language before being submerged or "transitioned" into the national language. In addition, I am in strong accord with the intent of his argument against utilizing superficial aspects of language proficiency as a basis for school placement or diagnosis of learning problems. Cummins (1982, 1984) has subsequently dropped the use of BICS and CALP as a result of discussions at the conference where this paper was given, and now employs a continuum from the context-embedded to context-reduced language interacting with a continuum of cognitively demanding to cognitively undemanding language. Nevertheless, many of the arguments herein are germane to his revised formulation.

2. The concept designated by the expression "knowledge of the world" is essentially problematic and rarely explicated. Presumably it consists largely of knowledge gained through participation in exposure to experiences typical of the middle class of the majority society. School rarely rewards knowledge gained through participation in activities typical of minority or lower SES groups (e.g. Taylor, 1977). (I am indebted to Benji Wald for bringing this issue to my attention.)

References

Abrahams, R. D. & Gay, G. 1972, Talking black in the classroom. In R. D. Abrahams & R. C. Troike (eds), *Language and cultural diversity in American education*. Englewood Cliffs, N.J.: Prentice-Hall, Inc.

Bamberger, R. 1973, Leading children to reading: An Austrian venture. In R. Karlin (ed.), *Reading for all*. Newark, Del.: International Reading Association.

Bernstein, B. 1975, *Class, codes and control: Theoretical studies towards a sociology of language*. New York: Schocken Books (Originally published: *Class, codes and control* Vol. 1. London: Routledge and Kegan Paul, 1971.

Bowles, S. & Gintis, H. 1976, *Schooling in capitalist America: Educational reform and the contradictions of economic life*. New York: Basic Books.

Carroll, J. 1979, Psychometric approaches to the study of language abilities. In C. J. Fillmore, D. Kempler, & W. S-Y. Wang (eds), *Individual differences in language ability and language behavior*. New York: Academic Press.

Cummins, J. 1979, Linguistic interdependence and the educational development of bilingual children. *Review of Educational Research* 49(2), 222–51.

— 1980a, The cross-lingual dimensions of language proficiency: Implications for bilingual education and the optimal age issue. *TESOL Quarterly*, 14(2), 175–88.

— 1980b, Psychological assessment of immigrant children: Logic or intuition? *Journal of Multilingual and Multicultural Development*, 1(2), 97–111.

— 1980c, The construct of language proficiency in bilingual education. In J. Alatis (ed.), *Current Issues in Bilingual Education*, Washington, D.C.: Georgetown University Press.

— 1982, The Role of Primary Language Development in Promoting Educational Success for Language Minority Students. In D. Dolson (ed.), *Schooling and Language Minority Students: A Theoretical Framework*. Sacramento, CA: California State Department of Education.

— 1984, Wanted: A Theoretical Framework for Relating Language Proficiency to Academic Achievement Among Bilingual Students. In C. Rivera (ed.) *Language Proficiency and Academic Achievement*. Clevedon, England: Multilingual Matters.

Cummins, J. & Swain, M. in press, Analysis by rhetoric: Reading the text or the reader's own projections: A reply to Edelsky *et al.*, *Applied Linguistics*.

Edelsky, C. & Hudelson, S. 1979, Resistance to the acquisition of Spanish by native English speakers in a bilingual setting. *Journal of the Linguistic Association of the Southwest*, 3(2), 102–111.

— 1980, Language acquisition and a marked language. *NABE Journal*, 5(1), 1–15.

Ilpola, P. 1979, Australian suomalainen arvostettu: Kieliolotkin kohentumassa [The Finns in Australia rated highly]. *Suomi Silta*, 2, 8–9.

Kimball, W. L. 1968, *Parent and family influences on academic achievement among Mexican American students*. Unpublished doctoral dissertation, University of California, Los Angeles.

Labov, W. 1969, The logic of nonstandard English. In J. Alatis (ed.) *Monograph series on languages and linguistics* (no. 22), Washington, D.C.: Georgetown University Press.

Lambert, W. E. 1975, Culture and language as factors in learning and education. In A. Wolfgang (ed.), *Education of immigrant students*. Toronto: Ontario Institute for Studies in Education.

Mace, B. J. 1972, *A linguistic profile of children entering Seattle public schools kindergartens in September, 1971, and implications for their instruction.* Unpublished master's thesis, University of Texas at Austin.

Mehan, H. 1979, *Learning lessons.* Cambridge, MA: Harvard University Press.

Moll, L. C., Estrada, E., Diaz, E. & Lopes, L. M. 1980, The organization of bilingual lessons: Implications for schooling. *The Quarterly Newsletter of the Laboratory of Comparative Human Cognition*, 2(3), 53–8.

Oller, J. 1978, The language factor in the evaluation of bilingual education. In J. Alatis (ed.), *International dimensions of bilingual education.* Washington, D.C.: Georgetown University Press.

Oller, J. W. 1980a, A language factor deeper than speech: More data and theory for bilingual assessment. In J. Alatis (ed.), *Current issues in bilingual education*, Washington, D.C.: Georgetown University Press.

— 1980b, A comment on specific variance versus global variance in certain EFL tests. *TESOL Quarterly* 14(4), 527–30.

Peale, E., & Lambert, W. 1962, The relation of bilingualism to intelligence. *Psychological Monographs*, 27(76), 1–23.

Platero, D. 1981, Personal communication.

Rickford, J. 1980, *Language attitudes in a creole continuum.* Paper presented at Linguistic Society of America annual meeting, San Antonio, TX, December.

Rosenthal, R. & Jakobson, L. 1968, *Pygmalion in the classroom: Teacher expectation and pupils' intellectual development.* New York: Holt, Rinehart and Winston.

Roth, D. 1974, Intelligence testing as a social activity. In A. Cicourel, K. Jennings, S. Jennings, K. Leiter, R. MacKay, H. Mehan & D. Roth (eds), *Language use and school performance.* New York: Academic Press.

Skutnabb-Kangas, T. & Toukomaa, P. 1976, *Teaching migrant children's mother tongue and learning the language of the host country in the context of the socio-cultural situation of the migrant family.* Tampere, Finnland: University of Tampere. (Department of Sociology and Social Psychology Research Report, 15, Box 601.)

Spearman, C. 1927, *Abilities of man: Their nature and measurement.* New York: Macmillan.

Swain, M. 1982, *Immersion education: Applicability for nonvernacular teaching to vernacular speakers.* In B. Hartford, A. Valdman and C. Foster (eds), *Issues in International Bilingual Education; The Role of the Vernacular.* New York: Plenum Press.

Taylor, O. 1977, The sociolinguistic dimension in standardized testing. In M. Saville-Troike (ed.), *Linguistics and anthropology: Georgetown University Round Table on Languages and Linguistics.* Washington, D.C.: Georgetown University Press.

Toukomaa, P. & Skutnabb-Kangas, T. 1977, The intensive teaching of the mother tongue to migrant children of pre-school age. Tampere, Finland: University of Tampere (Dept. of Sociology and Social Psychology Research Report 26).

Troike, R. 1978, Research evidence for the effectiveness of bilingual education. *NABE Journal*, 3(1), 13–24.

— 1981, A synthesis of research on bilingual education. *Educational Leadership* 14(38), 498–504.

Upshur, J. A. 1973, Context for language testing. In J. Oller & J. C. Richards (eds), *Focus on the learner: Pragmatic perspectives for the language teacher.* Rowley, MA: Newbury House.

Vellutino, F. R. 1977, Alternative conceptualizations of dyslexia: Evidence in support of a verbal deficit hypothesis. *Harvard Educational Review*, 47, 334–54.
— 1979, *Dyslexia: Theory and research*. Cambridge, MA: MIT Press.
Williams, F. 1976, *Explorations of the linguistic attitudes of teachers*. Rowley, MA: Newbury House.
Willis, P. 1977, *Learning to labour: How working class kids get working class jobs.* Lexington, MA: Lexington Books.
Wong-Fillmore, L. 1976, *The second time around: Cognitive and social strategies in second language acquisition*. Unpublished doctoral dissertation, Stanford University.

A sociolinguistic perspective on Cummins' current framework for relating language proficiency to academic achievement

Benji Wald
National Center for Bilingual Research

The purpose of this paper is to interpret Cummin's current framework for relating language proficiency to academic achievement among bilingual students from a sociolinguistic perspective. The basic framework has proven to be both powerful in its durability and responsive to sociolinguistic considerations. The intention here is to recognize the strengths that account for its power, both in terms of its internal consistency and in relation to other theories, as well as to indicate some of its limitations and possible misinterpretations of the development and use of language in social contexts. In particular, concern will be expressed about its ability to make contact between the overall language resources of minority language students, within the school and without, and the specific language proficiencies which are most relevant to academic achievement.

Cummins' discussion of the evolution of the current framework shows a sensitivity to socially rooted issues. However, this is not always made explicit. The relatively minor role of the threshold hypotheses in the current framework is an example.

The early and late threshold hypotheses of linguistic proficiency have not turned out to be particularly useful in accounting for the difference in outcomes of majority immersion programs and the nearest practised equivalent of minority submersion, both featuring instruction in a second language at the outset of schooling. This may account for why they have not been prominently pursued in the context of the education of minority language students. The threshold hypotheses are related to "critical age" hypotheses which have been used to address the issue of the allegedly beneficial and/or noxious effects of early bilingualism. While this is of intrinsic theoretical interest and practical concern to creating bilinguals out of majority monolinguals, and/or of maintaining community-based bilingualism and cultivating it for academic purposes, it is not of immediate relevance to minority students who first come to school either as bilinguals or as minority language monolinguals, and are then subjected to programs intended to transition them to the majority language. This is the type of program that Cummins addresses in terms of entry/exit criteria for bilingual education. This type of program is the reality in many U.S. state and local school districts for Hispanic students, most of whom are from lower-than-middle socio-economic backgrounds, resident in highly segregated neighborhoods, and conversant in a socio-cultural system including language forms and uses different from and often stigmatized by the norms of the school system (academically, the stigmatized forms are often called "errors" and the stigmatized uses "bad", "antisocial" or "inappropriate" verbal behavior). This situation applies to the forms of Spanish as well as English normally used by these students (e.g. for the chasm between literary and vernacular forms of Spanish see, for example, Valdés et al., 1981).

Sociolinguistic research has uncovered massive evidence that wherever socio-economic class structure is discernible, it is reflected in language distinctions, and that the educational system tends to positively value the language features and other behavioral patterns resembling those of the higher classes, and to devalue those of the lower classes (cf. Shuy & Fasold, 1973). Historically, extreme forms of stigma applied to the Spanish of these students in many U.S. educational systems have included punishment for speaking the language on school grounds, often in the form of detention, a general penalty also applied to persistent but not totally disruptive nonlinguistic behavioral infractions of the school code of conduct (cf. discussion in Peñalosa, 1980). More insidious was application of the same classifications and methods of treatment for minority language monolinguals and bilinguals of perceived limited English ability with no known learning disorders in their first language as for majority monolinguals with known learning disorders. Bilingual education of any form represents an advance over these unsuccessful methods by recognizing the need for an initial common language for many of the communicative interactions which must take place between students and school personnel, particularly teachers and aides in instructional settings.

This historical and social context confounds the abstract relation of language proficiency to academic achievement with the reality of social stigma for the majority of language minority students. A theory which seeks to offer concrete suggestions for improving the academic performance of these students will have to integrate this context into its framework.

Both the terms *language proficiency* and *academic achievement* bear further scrutiny. This section will be concerned mainly with the notion language proficiency. In the ensuing discussion it will become clear that Cummins' notion of academic achievement is precisely equivalent to the acquisition of literacy skills.

In discussing language proficiency assessment in bilingual programs, Cummins points out the confused state of the art. This is understandable since the mediating effect of language in all social and academic situations is complex and pervasive. However, no matter how language proficiency is subcategorized in theory, in practice the actual assessment of all its components are closely associated with the measurement of language performance in test situations. In order to avoid terminological confusion in the ensuing discussion, this state of affairs will be acknowledged by reserving the term "language proficiency" exclusively for *test language*, meaning the language performance of students in response to a test situation, whether spoken or written. This will serve as a point of contrast with *spontaneous language*, meaning the language performance of speakers in face-to-face communicative contexts. All language behavior, whether in a test or any other situation, and the knowledge of language forms and uses underlying this behavior will simply be referred to as language abilities, skills or resources (cf. Wald, 1981a, 1981b).

In the senses defined above, the distinction between what Labov and Shuy, on the one hand, and Oller and Perkins, on the other, are talking about can be made easier to understand (see references in Cummins, this volume). Labov and Shuy are not talking about language proficiency, but rather about the falseness of associating nonstandard, often stigmatized, forms of language with cognitive deficiencies in their speakers, and the attempt of some educators to use the argument of cognitive deficit to account for the speakers' depressed academic achievement. On the contrary, they are proposing that the stigma and subtler forms of negative evaluation of minority students' linguistic behavior have *social* consequences in student-teacher and student-test interaction that lead to depressed academic achievement, an aggravated classroom situation, truancy, and possible dropping out of school at an early age. Their objective has been to call attention to the common confusion between cognition and social prejudice (whether conscious or not) in the hypotheses of many educational psychologists.

The enterprise of Oller and Perkins, and others concerned with formal language testing, is quite different. That some forms of test language behavior correlate more closely with achievement (literacy) and I.Q. (verbal?) than others is the origin of Cummins' polarization of BICS and CALP, as will be discussed below. However, first it is necessary to address his potentially misleading representation of the concerns of sociolinguistic ethnographers.

In discussing the views of ethnographers concerned with the relation of the communicative demands of everyday situations (of which those called "natural face-to-face situations" by Cummins are particularly prominent) to classroom situations, Cummins does not accurately present the motivation and scope of that research. The school ethnographers are concerned with all aspects of linguistic behavior in the classroom, and elsewhere in the social territory. Naturally, early efforts have focussed to a large extent on student-teacher interaction in instructional settings. A common finding has been a wide variety of mismatches between the systems of language forms and uses of minority students and of the teachers. While stigma was mentioned above, mutual ignorance leading to misinterpretation of similar forms but with different uses across systems has also been uncovered. A classic example, first suggested by Labov, involves the misinterpretation of pronunciation as a decoding error. Thus, for speakers first learning how to read, teachers may misinterpret a pronunciation difference as a decoding error, e.g. when *mist* is pronounced as *mis'* (misinterpreted as *miss*, a different word). The difference between the original and the corrected pronunciation may either not be perceived at all by the student, or not considered relevant to the task s/he thought s/he was supposed to perform. In either case, confusion or discouragement from the reading process may result. In this concrete case, pronunciation may end up seriously affecting the growth of literacy skills. Such examples abound in the sociolinguistic literature on the effects of nonstandard language and other forms of behaviour in the classroom and fit into the larger scheme of cross-linguistic miscommunications developed by Gumperz and Hymes (cf. Hymes, 1971, 1980; Gumperz & Herasimchuk, 1975, Gumperz, 1981). Very much akin to the specific example given above are Moll's (1981) observations of the exaggerated attention paid to pronunciation in English of Hispanic third graders highly skilled in Spanish reading.

Cummins' example of the girl of ESL background, who was not so perceived by her teacher and a school psychologist, may be another example of misintepretation of linguistic behavior. Although Cummins uses the example to suggest that fluency (itself an unclear notion, as discussed later) masks a deeper level of second language underdevelopment observable only through test performance, the details of the anecdote may also suggest that the girl talked very little at all (and certainly did not use her first language). According to this interpretation, the psychologist misinterpreted her observed suppression of language as a low degree of general verbality, supported by her low tested (English) verbal IQ. The social dimension missing from both the psychologist's and her teacher's recorded observations is how verbal the girl is in either her first or second language in any non-school context. Although subtler forms of stigma may have been operant in the girl's suppression of her first language (at least within earshot of the teacher), it is likely that the same observations would be made of Hispanics of limited English ability who suppressed Spanish on school territory under pain of detention (or simply embarrassment).

The evidence of sociolinguistic ethnography in support of cross-linguistic miscommunication of all types suggests that the match of language form and function in everyday situations to the system required in the classroom is very much involved in the outcome of academic achievement. While Cummins may be right in denying that some of these behaviors have a *direct* relation to literacy level, he must not ignore that they are preconditions to any kind of academic achievement by influencing the morale of the students in interaction with the teacher, as well as by shaping the teacher's expectations of the students' capabilities according to the self-fulfilling prophesy hypothesis. Especially when teachers and students do not share the same set of norms for communication, and are subject to mutual sociocultural ignorance — a particularly common occurence with language minority students — the emphasis on developing "proficiency" in processing written text will almost certainly be a frustrating one for many students and their teachers.[1]

Cummins' failure to recognize the fundamental point of the relevance of natural face-to-face situations to classroom interaction and academic achievement, reflects the basic isolation of psychological theories from sociolinguistic and ethnographic research, despite his brief acknowledgments of the mitigating effects of social context on the development of literacy skills.

The CALP-BICS distinction will now be discussed in pursuit of further clarification of the basic concepts of language proficiency and academic achievement. This will prepare the way for discussion of the futher transformation of these notions in the current framework.

It becomes increasingly clear in Cummins' development of the CALP concept that it is a measure of literacy itself, and not simply of the preconditions for literacy in speech. Since CALP skills are strictly test skills, one may see that the notion of academic achievement is reflected, indeed measured, in both literacy and test-taking skills. A literate person with no test-taking skills cannot be recognized by any measures associated with CALP, and is probably an impossibility in principle. At the same time it is doubtful that illiterates can do well on written cloze tests, dictation and other measures of CALP that require literacy. The manipulations of language of oral cloze tests and other CALP measures such as amount of literate vocabulary (as opposed to vernacular, non-academic vocabulary) are school tasks without necessary analogs in everyday language behavior. The type of training which develops these oral test-taking skills appears to be closely related to the training which develops literacy. However, the more precise connection is not clear in Cummins' framework. It would seem more likely that high scores on oral CALP measures proceed from literacy rather than the other way around, but this remains to future research on the mechanics, rather than simply the statistical correlation, of the relation of literacy to oral test-taking.

Until further clarifications are made, it would be easier to understand CALP as literacy skills, rather than as some more profound psychological construct involving some less well understood form of cognition not attributable to illiterates. The reformulation of CALP as relatively context-reduced and cognitively demanding uses of language confirms the interpretation that it is fundamentally addressed to literacy rather than the social preconditions for learning. This will be discussed in the next section.

According to Cummins' earlier schemata, CALP contrasts with BICS. As Cummins notes, the terms behind the acronym BICS, perhaps along with the perception that CALP is something like literacy, misled many scholars into associating BICS with all language skills which were not directly or demonstrably related to literacy, in particular any interactive form of speech behavior in a non-academic situation. In discussing the current framework, Cummins clarifies that BICS refers to aspects of language proficiency which are characterized as "saliently rapidly developed aspects of communicative proficiency, e.g. accent, fluency". In the larger context of Cummins' work, BICS refers to aspects of language which develop quickly in the first language and the second language of *young* bilinguals (pre-adolescents), but not necessarily among adolescents or adults first exposed to a second language in either an academic or natural social milieu. Since, as Cummins has observed, young children tend to acquire fluency and native-like pronunciation of second languages, but that these do not appear to correlate with academic achievement, he distinguishes them from CALP. And for good reason, since older speakers (take college students, for example) do not need to learn native pronunciation or to speak fluently in order to read and write a new language (this is particularly obvious in the learning of dead languages such as Latin and Ancient Greek).

As an example of a BICS skill, the notion of "fluency" will be discussed here in greater detail.

In discussing exit criteria, Cummins represents the literature as suggesting that fluency in a second language is attained relatively quickly by young "immigrant" students. However, the literature cited does not precisely specify what fluency is. Elsewhere Cummins suggests that it may be defined in terms of words per unit time (Cummins, 1980, p. 178). However, this is inaccurate since it implies that faster speakers are more fluent than slower speakers regardless of the reasons for the difference in their tempos, and that speakers who use longer words are less fluent than speakers who use shorter words speaking at the same tempo. This is certainly not the basis upon which judgments of fluency in a second language are made. Thus, it is unclear what basis is used for impressionistic ratings of fluency, and consequently, how to explain its lack of correlation with literacy. The claim that second language fluency is generally achieved in one and a half to two years does not correspond to the behavioral characteristics observed for 10–12 year old Mexican American children in the Los Angeles area. Quite generally, it has been found that students of less than four to five years residence in an English-speaking environment preferred Spanish in spontaneous conversation, and have difficulty in competing for the floor in English with age-mates of earlier ages of arrival (Wald, 1981c). In this case, it is evident that there are social interactive skills in non-test situations which allow inferences about readiness to exit to an English-only program. This indicates that impressions of fluency are not only vague but observationally inadequate for assessing a student's second language skills. Spontaneous speech behavior in peer-interactive situations is an indicator of language abilities of far greater observational adequacy than tests of "fluency".

Fluency is representative of the set of BICS-classified skills exemplified by Cummins. The others appear to be pronunciation and oral comprehension. They are not well-defined, are invariably rated impressionistically, and are based on test situations rather than on spontaneous speech, the last being the only example of a feature they share with CALP measures as elements of language proficiency. In contrast with socially functional speech behavior in interactive situations, test speech behavior is of dubious meaningfulness to the students required to perform in test situations, and impressionistic ratings are known to be subject to social prejudices, as mentioned earlier. Cummins does the educational process a service in pointing out the unreliability of these forms of language proficiency toward the understanding of academic achievement, but he would do great harm to suggest that as BICS these forms of test language are representative in any clear way of natural functional speech behavior.

Cummins suggests that the CALP-BICS distinction has been subject to a great deal of misunderstanding involving the referents of those terms. His former models presented a sharp boundary between CALP and BICS (either in the form of a water-line or as the intersection of two circles). This boundary reflected the criterial boundary between proficiency tests and language skills which correlated highly with measures of literacy, and all other language skills. Hesitation over whether listening comprehension should be classified as CALP or BICS according to the given criteria supported the impression of a dichotomy (Cummins, 1980, p. 180). Since all language skills were measured in test language, how to interpret these constructs as they related to language in general, and particularly to language skills exhibited in non-test situations became an underlying issue for sociolinguists. A common misunderstanding might be that BICS extends to all interactive speech (including spontaneous speech), in all situations, since CALP has only been recognized in test language.

The current framework implicitly addresses that problem and introduces a new set of issues.

The new framework no longer restricts itself to test language, but anecdotally includes features of language in interactive contexts. It weds the seemingly social concept of context-embedding with the psychological concept of cognitive demand (apparently, mental effort). According to the framework, any language skill, whether in a test situation or otherwise, can theoretically be measured simultaneously along these two dimensions (as if they were co-ordinates of a Cartesian graph). The framework is not developed to the point of suggesting how to measure. To some extent this is due to an inherent unclarity in the concepts themselves, at least as currently presented. In any event, this state of affairs creates difficulty in interpreting language behavior, whether in a test situation or otherwise, in accordance with the framework. This is discussed below.

The use of continua intends to represent progressive development along the two dimensions of context-embeddedness and cognitive demand. These two concepts and the linearity of the model are discussed in turn.

Cummins' concept of context-embedding, or context in general, as it applies to the role of language in communication, is clear only for extreme cases. A number of features of context which are distinguished by sociolinguists are collapsed into a single linear model. For example, face-to-face communication, as Cummins notes, avails itself of a number of cues beyond the basic representations of written language (but possible to annotate in choreography, stage directions, etc.), that is, intonation, gesture, posture, proximity and other actively communicative (changeable) features of a social context. However, to what extent these forms of communication support a linguistic message in a way that they must be transformed into written linguistic units in the "explicitness" of idealized written communication is far from clear.

Most of Cummins' discussion of context is addressed to a very specific element of context which he labels "shared reality". This construct is the static reflection of the sociolinguistic concept of "shared knowledge". Like other examples of actively communicative features accompanying speech in interpersonal situations, it is changeable. However, whereas gesture, posture, etc. change from one signal to another, shared knowledge is *cumulative*. Unlike the other features accompanying speech, it is also found in school readers, as in every use of language. A great deal of confusion, if not downright inaccuracy, is found in the accounts of "context" by educational psychologists. The non-discrimination between the linguistic aspects of shared knowledge and nonlinguistic kinesic elements in face-to-face communication is a crucial case in point. The possible implication that the interpersonal construct of shared knowledge (or "shared reality") is minimized in written communication as opposed to face-to-face interaction would be false.

This implication is worth discussing in some detail since it rests on two stereotypes commonly accepted in educational psychology. The first is that interactive communication is primarily driven by immediate instrumental motives and is concerned with features of the immediate environment. Most of the evidence for this stereotype comes from limited observations of very young, especially pre-school, children (e.g. Wells, 1981a). The second is that complex written communication, especially of the academic type, is maximally explicit and minimally dependent on "context". It will become clear that in this case "context" does not refer to shared knowledge but rather to the physical context in which the printed material is embedded, e.g. the quality of the paper it is written on, the color of the cover, or any feature of the transient condition of the reader (sitting, lying down, engaged, frowning, yawning, etc.).

With regard to complex written communication, the notion that it is only minimally context-embedded ignores the cumulative nature of learning in general, and of reading comprehension in particular. For example, an intermediate or advanced book in history, psychology, etc. would be more context-embedded than an introductory text. The high number of referents in learned prose which are presupposed by an author to be familiar to the reader has been measured by Prince (1981). The work of Fillmore & Kay (1980) on the protocols through which elementary school children form expectations early in the process of reading a text and the bases on which they make decisions in selecting among multiple choice answers to reading comprehension tasks, indicate that reading comprehension invariably proceeds by integrating the information expressed in the text with "knowledge of the world". To the extent that knowledge of the world presupposed by the text is culturally determined, a member of a different background may not have the knowledge necessary to understand the text. This problem is the same as cultural bias in testing, and is by no means a purely linguistic problem. Texts presupposing knowledge of Mexico City, and certainly Madrid, may be as puzzling to Los Angeles Spanish speakers as texts presupposing knowledge of "Main Street, U.S.A.".

As a result of unclarities about the elements of context in the current model, the continuous nature of context-embedded language does not clearly or helpfully express the relation of written to spoken language. Thus, in the examples given by Cummins, "engaging in a discussion" is considered more context-embedded than the examples given of written language. However, it would seem that if "shared reality" were criterial of context-embeddedness, an intense interactive academic discussion might be more similar to the amount of context involved in "writing (or reading) an academic article" than to "writing a letter to a close friend".

With regard to the stereotype that interactive speech is highly dependent on on-going activities of immediate concern and physical props embedded in the speech situation, part of this notion may derive from Wells' (1981a) study of the interactive behavior of pre-schoolers with adult care-givers, and their subsequent literacy skills in the low grades of elementary school. Wells notes that, as a group, children who were read stories in their pre-school years tended to achieve literacy skills faster than the others. He adopted the notion that the cause of this differential rate of acquisition of literacy skills was prior familiarity of the faster learners with "decontextualized" language (cf. Wells, 1981b). However, Wells does not note whether differential exposure to oral stories, narratives or gossip, which are equivalently decontextualized (in the sense of referring to objects, people and situations not observable in the speech context), also correlates with a faster rate of literacy achievement. If it does, then the notion that pre-school practice in "decontextualization" contributes to literacy receives support. If not, then there are many other features of reading situations that can be brought to bear on the achievement of the youngsters, e.g. the style of language used in books (cf. Green, 1981), or simply advance exposure to the relation between reading and talking, e.g. that the vowel of *the* can be pronounced in the same way as the vowel of *me* (rarely found in spontaneous speech but common in reading out loud).

Some indication of confusion in developing the notion of context for his own purposes is evident in Cummins' characterization of context-reduction as relying primarily on linguistic cues and even in some cases "suspending knowledge of the real world in order to interpret (or manipulate) the logic of the communication appropriately". These characteristics are also common to many forms of oral communication, e.g. as mentioned immediately above, oral stories, jokes, narratives of personal experience, reports about what somebody else did, etc., rely primarily on linguistic cues. They are certainly within the competence of mid to late pre-adolescents, who are able to produce and understand narratives of personal experience (without supporting props) in at least one language. Similarly, these children are capable of hypothetical discourse of the type "what if....?", "let's pretend...", etc. These uses of language involve suspending knowledge of the "real" world. Furthermore, none of these skills presuppose literacy, as they are commonly observed in preliterate societies. A basic question which needs to be answered for the current framework's concept of context is: are such context-reduced communications still more context-embedded than any form of written language simply by virtue of their face-to-face behavioral setting?

Cummins' concept of cognitive demand or involvement is relatively clear as an aspect of learning in which a language skill becomes increasingly automatized so that ultimately the speed with which it is processed is maximized. However, Cummins' characterization of first and second language skills as showing the same progression in development is grossly misleading. This cannot even be intended since it conflicts with the interdependence hypothesis if taken literally.

Setting aside the distinction between literacy-related and other language skills (according to Cummins' hypotheses) for the moment, the role of transfer in second language acquisition is far from settled (cf. Krashen & Scarcella, 1980). Transfer appears to differentially affect different components of the second language. To be sure, research has amply demonstrated that some aspects of morphology show similar orders of acquisition in first and second languages (but see Hatch, 1978, especially articles by Hakuta and Ravem on first language effects on L2). The same can be said of phonology and syntax. That is, to the extent that features of those aspects of language are acquired relatively late by first language learners, they are also acquired late by second language learners, if (and this is the crucial "if") they are not already present in the first language, e.g. in English phonology, the difference between *then* and *den*; in English syntax, the form and placement of verbal negation. The evidence of research on both second language acquisition and unstable pidgins indicates that in phonology and syntax at the sentence level, there is an interaction between transfer and first-language-like processes of development. Older speakers, without explicit instruction, fail to acquire certain characteristics of monolingual speech in the second language, but rather (1) continue to use features resembling earlier stages of first language acquisition and (2) continue to use features resembling those of their first languages (cf. Bickerton & Odo, 1976). Pre-adolescent speakers acquire the general, if not specific, features of the vernacular (everyday) form of the second language to which they are exposed (cf. Payne, 1980; Wald, 1981c).

It is not clear to what extent cognitive demand is involved in the processes of second language acquisition in natural contexts. Cummins' notions about first language acquisition are purely speculative in suggesting that the cognitive demands of a child learning a first language are greater below the age of three than above it — and on into adulthood. In both phonology and syntax, development will depend on social conditions. Late prestige variants in both phonology and syntax are acquired with great difficulty if at all. Some of the features of socio-economic class distinctions in a society arise through differential access to these features according to class. Thus, New Yorkers raised in the r-less vernacular of New York City rarely learn to use syllable-final consonantal *r*, as in *car*, etc., with total consistency (cf. Labov, 1972b).

With regard to second language acquisition, which in principle is not qualitatively different from learning different styles and registers in a first language, a commonly observed pattern is lack of distinction at the first stage, followed by hypercorrection of the new form involved in the distinction at the second stage, and then gradual consistency in maintaining the distinction as in the target system, e.g. the development of subject-auxiliary inversion in main and embedded wh- questions, e.g. *where do you live*, with inversion, but *he asked me where I live(d)*, without inversion in standard written English (cf. Schumann, 1978; Cazden, Cancino, Rosansky, Schumann, 1975: further analysis and discussion are found in Wald, 1981d). Is it meaningful to ask whether the second or third stage is cognitively more demanding?

Whether or not equations between cognitive demand in academic and in non-academic contexts can be made will depend on whether empirical techniques of measurement can be devised for this construct. If so, it may be possible to recognize and transfer demanding behavior from a natural context to an academic one. If not, it is not clear how to proceed in developing literacy skills on the basis of the notion of cognitive demand.

Cummins identifies a particularly cognitively demanding task in persuading a colleague that one's point of view is valid in an academic context. However, the concept is not sufficiently developed to evaluate whether that example is more or less cognitively demanding than Labov's well-known example of Larry H's interactive argument about the color of God (Labov, 1972a, p. 241ff). Labov's intention was to show that clarity and logic can be expressed in non-academic contexts and with the use of nonstandard language forms, with apparent ease by a 16 year-old with a second grade reading level. A very serious problem for the education of members of minority groups living under segregated and historically stigmatized conditions is: can these highly developed skills existing in natural social contexts be adopted to school achievement?

According to the view presented here, this question has implications for the relation of the context/cognition aspects of the framework to the interdependence hypothesis. In the current formulation, the interdependence hypothesis is not integrated into the context/cognition hypothesis, but rather exists as an independent consideration. The gist of the interdependence hypothesis is that literacy skills that have developed in one language can be transferred to a second language. However, this is essentially viewed as a passive process. The demanding part of the process, as currently represented, exists in developing the literacy skills in any language. Is this cognitively demanding only for the student, or also for the reading instructor?

While there is much reason to believe that some form of the interdependence hypothesis is accurate on the observational level (cf. the comments above about learning Latin and Ancient Greek), and that Cummins' recommendations are reasonable and logical given the current state of knowledge of the preconditions for academic achievement, most of the serious work remains to be done in clarifying and operationalizing the current underpinnings of the framework with its constructs of context and cognitive demand. This is especially important in evaluating oral language proficiency instruments according to Cummins' recommendations for entry criteria, i.e. "the assessment procedures for entry purposes should involve cognitively-demanding context-embedded measures which are fair to the variety of L1 (and L2) spoken by the child" (p. 16). It seems clear that in this passage "context-embedded" means "oral" or "speech". "Cognitively-demanding" seems to exclude "fluency" and other measures which, as mentioned are impressionistic, vague and observationally inadequate. However, if "cognitively-demanding" presupposes literacy, as suggested above, what is left for preliterate students?

In addition, unless the actual process involved in interdependence of literacy skills across languages can be understood, it will not be clear whether human intervention can aid in facilitating this process. If it can, then the possibility of adapting non-academic "cognitively demanding" uses of language to develop equivalent academic skills will emerge. If not, then the only practical consequences of the hypothesis may be that language minority students will be kept in first language classes until they achieve a certain level of literacy (40th percentile of national, state or local monolingual English norms according to the system operant in California, for example), or drop out of school.

The importance of taking into account the social context in which all of these more abstract considerations are functioning can be appreciated by considering that in some bilingual communities, at the same time that academic skills may be developing in the classroom in first languages (non-English), social pressures, not all of which are clearly of school origin, are pulling students toward the use of English to the extent that they can manage it. Thus, while preferences for Spanish were observed for 11–12 year olds of lengths of residence of less than five years, English was characteristically preferred by speakers of longer exposure to the English environment of both the school and age-mates in the community. In some cases, English was sufficiently developed for peer interaction without any discernible inequities of a linguistic nature, and Spanish language behavior could be elicited only with great difficulty because of the social circumstances, but was found to be well developed. In some other cases, the preference for English existed despite greater ability to compete in conversation in Spanish (Wald, 1981c). At that point, motivational factors in the further academic development of Spanish may come into play in a negative fashion.

In sum, Cummins' theoretical framework goes a long way in imposing order on the multiplicity of observations and proposals concerning the relation of language proficiency to academic achievement. The issues his framework has raised, and its general capacity for enrichment, account for a great deal of its durability. However, unless some of the basic concepts discussed above are refined for further clarity and informed by the specific socio-cultural settings in which many lower SES bilingual and non-English monolingual communities are situated, including the forms and uses of language in non-academic contexts, the framework will remain an academic abstraction incapable of making contact between the language resources developing among the students independently of academic contexts and the development of literacy skills necessary for academic achievement.

Note

1. The example of misinterpretation of phonology as discussed above is particularly revealing. In fact, it seems that much evidence is converging on the need to de-emphasize the phonics approach in reading for two reasons: (1) practicality; due to the great variation in the pronunciation of monolingual dialects of English, let alone the English of second language speakers, and the general lack of consistency of English orthography (from the point of view of any current dialect of English, including the standard), (2) lack of necessity; reactions against heavy reliance on phonics, i.e. the "bottom-up theory" of learning to read, are reflected in "top-down" and integrative theories of reading.

References

Bickerton, D. & Odo, C. 1976, *Change and variation in Hawaiian English* (Vol. 1) (NSF Final Rep.; Project No. GS-39748). University of Hawaii.
Cazden, C., Cancino, H., Rosansky, E. & Schumann, J. 1975, Second language acquisition sequences in children, adolescents and adults (NIE Final Rep.; Project No. 730744). Washington, D.C.: National Institute of Education.
Cummins, J. 1980, The cross-lingual dimensions of language proficiency: Implications for bilingual education and the optimal age issue. *TESOL Quarterly*, 14(2), 175–87.
Fillmore, C. & Kay, P. 1980, *Progress report: Test semantic analysis of reading comprehension tests*. Unpublished report, University of California at Berkely, Departments of Linguistics and Anthropology.
Green, G. 1981, Competence for implicit text analysis: Literary style discrimination in five year olds. *Studies in the Linguistic Sciences*, 11(2), 39–56.
Gumperz, J. J. 1981, *Urban Communication and Social Inequality*. Papers presented at the 80th Annual Meeting of the American Anthropological Association, Los Angeles, December.
Gumperz, J. J. & Herasimchuk, E. 1975, The conversational analysis of social meaning: A study of classroom interaction. In M. Sanchez & B. Blount (eds), *Sociocultural dimensions of language use*. New York: Academic Press.
Hatch, E. (ed.), 1978, *Second language acquisition: A book of readings*. Rowley, Mass.: Newbury House.
Hymes, D. 1971, Bilingual education: Linguistic and sociolinguistic bases. In J. E. Alatis (ed.), *Bilingualism and language contact: Anthropological, linguistic, psychological, and social aspects. 21st Annual Round Table: Monograph Series on Language and Linguistics*.
— 1980, *Language in education: Ethnolinguistic essays*. Washington, D.C.: Center for Applied Linguistics.
Krashen, S. & Scarcella, R. (eds), 1980, *Research in second language acquisition*. Rowley, Mass.: Newbury House.
Labov, W. 1972a, *Language in the inner city: Studies in the Black English Vernacular*. Philadelphia: University of Pennsylvania Press.
— 1972b, *Sociolinguistic patterns*. Philadelphia: University of Pennsylvania Press.
Moll, L. 1981, The microethnographic study of bilingual schooling. In R. V. Padilla (ed.), *Bilingual education technology: Ethnoperspectives in bilingual education research* (Vol. 3). Ypsilanti: Eastern Michigan University.
Payne, A. 1980, Factors controlling the acquisition of the Philadelphia dialect by out of state children. In W. Labov (ed.), *Locating language in time and space*. New York: Academic Press.
Peñalosa, F. 1980, *Chicano sociolinguistics: An introduction*. Rowley, Mass.: Newbury House.
Prince, E. 1981, Toward a taxonomy of given – new information. In P. Cole (ed.), *Radical pragmatics*. New York: Academic Press.
Schumann, J. 1978, *The pidginization process: A model for second language acquisition*. Rowley, Mass.: Newbury House.
Shuy, R. W. & Fasold, R. W. (ed.), 1973, *Language attitudes: Current trends and prospects*. Washington, D.C.: Georgetown University School of Languages and Linguistics.
Valdés, G., Lozano, A. G. & Garcia – Moya, R. (eds), 1981, *Teaching Spanish to the*

Hispanic bilingual: Issues, aims, and methods. New York: Teachers College Press.

Wald, B. 1981a, The relation of topic/situation sensitivity to the study of language prociciency. In. R. Padilla (ed.), *Bilingual education technology: Ethnoperspectives in bilingual education research* (Vol. 3). Ypsilanti: Eastern Michigan University.

— 1981b, *On assessing the oral language ability of limited English proficient students: The linguistic bases of the non-comparability of different language proficiency assessment measures.* In S. S. Seidner (ed.). *Issues of Language Assessment. Foundations and Research,* 117–126. Evanston, Ill.: Illinois State Board of Education.

— 1981c, *Topic and situation as factors in language performance* NIE Final Report). Los Alamitos: National Center for Bilingual Research.

— 1981d, *The status of Chicano English as a dialect of American English.* Forthcoming in J. Ornstein-Galicia & J. Penfield (eds) Form and function in Chicano English. Rowley, Mass: Newbury House.

Wells, G. 1981a, *Learning through inter-action: The study of language development.* Cambridge: Oxford University Press.

— 1981b, *Preschool literacy related activities and success in school.* Manuscript submitted for publication.

Language proficiency and academic achievement revisited: A response

Jim Cummins
The Ontario Institute for Studies in Education

My purpose in this brief response is to try to clarify some aspects of the theoretical framework which has been the subject of very constructive criticism in the preceding chapters. The principal concern that emerges is the perception that the role of social factors in explaining differential school success has been neglected in comparison to the role assigned to cognitive/linguistic factors. I shall comment first on this issue and then consider some of the more specific concerns raised by individual authors.

The social context of schooling

The issues raised about social factors fall into two broad categories. First, both Genesee and Troike argue that language and cognitive variables are insufficient to account for differential school progress in bilingual situations. Troike suggests that both social and cultural factors may be more powerful than purely linguistic factors in influencing achievement while Genesee argues that the language proficiencies discussed in the framework "may best be conceived as intervening effects rather than as causal factors".

In response to these concerns it should be noted that the cognitive/linguistic proficiencies postulated at various stages in the evolution of the framework have always been identified as intervening variables rather than as independent causal variables. The point of the *interaction model* of bilingual education (Cummins, 1979) was that conceptual/linguistic skills and knowledge develop in particular socio-cultural contexts as a function of interpersonal experiences and interact with educational treatments to produce academic outcomes. Although the focus in several articles was primarily on these intervening variables, the role of social variables was also explicitly considered (e.g. Cummins, 1980, 1981a, 1981b). The most complete discussion of the role of sociopolitical factors is in Cummins (1982a), where the notion of "bicultural ambivalence" is related to Ogbu's (1978) distinction between "caste", "immigrant" and "autonomous" minorities. In short, the causal primacy of sociopolitical factors is not in question; however, cognitive and linguistic factors are also of obvious relevance to consider as intervening variables in interaction with educational treatment. The equally poor school performance of blacks in comparison to Hispanics, as suggested by Troike, certainly constitutes an explanatory problem for the "linguistic mismatch" hypothesis which unfortunately most proponents of bilingual education appear to endorse; however, the present framework evolved explicitly in opposition to the linguistic mismatch hypothesis and appears capable of accounting for the data discussed by Troike (see Cummins, 1979, 1981b, 1982a).

The second set of concerns about the role of social factors relates to the specific role of sociolinguistic factors and the meaning of the term "context" in the context-embedded/context-reduced continuum. This issue is discussed in most detail by Wald but is also raised by Canale, Genesee and Troike. Wald's point, which is clearly valid, is that "a number of features of context which are distinguished by sociolinguists are collapsed into a single linear model". All four authors point out that "shared knowledge" or familiarity and acceptance of various language tasks are equally important aspects of academic ("context-reduced") as well as of non-academic ("context-embedded") tasks.

A possible means of addressing the vagueness and ambiguity in the notion of "contextual support" is to distinguish between internal and external context. External context refers to aspects of language activities or tasks which are more or less objectively specifiable along the embedded-reduced continuum. Thus, by their nature, literacy activities tend to be more context-reduced than face-to-face communication because the message (meaning) is carried by a smaller *range* of cues. However, the location of any particular task on the continuum will be greatly influenced by internal contextual factors such as degree of familiarity and acceptance of the task/activity. The same considerations apply to the vertical continuum.

A similar point was made in Cummins (1981b) in discussing the framework:

"Thus, an important characteristic of the theoretical framework is that although communicative tasks and activities can be mapped onto it in a general way (e.g. inherent text characteristics make reading and writing less context-embedded than face-to-face communication), the exact location of any particular task on the horizontal and vertical continuums will depend on the individual's or group's proficiency level and acquisition context" (1981b, p. 14).

Thus, although sociolinguistic factors are not discussed in detail in relation to the framework, it appears capable of accomodating the important and myriad influences of these factors. Recall also that the entire framework is regarded as a set of intervening variables; thus, there is no inherent difficulty in postulating that sociolinguistic factors affect teacher-pupil interactions which, in turn, affect the development of literacy skills. Thus, as pointed out by McLaughlin (1982) and the authors in the present volume, relatively context-embedded interactions will affect the acquisition of literacy-related language skills in the classroom. This has been expressed in the context of the framework with reference to Wells' (1981) research as well as with reference to the major pedagogical implication that the more context-embedded the initial input (e.g. in L1 literacy instruction or L2 teaching) the more successful it will be in developing context-reduced language and literacy skills (see Cummins, 1981b, 1982b).

In summary, the papers in the present volume have correctly pointed to the fact that the role of sociolinguistic factors within the current framework requires clarification and elaboration. Within the boundaries of the issues to which the framework is addressed, I believe that these factors can be incorporated in more detail than has been the case up to now without relinquishing the parsimony of two basic dimensions.

Some specific points

"Basic" language proficiency

Canale suggests that we need to posit "language related universals" that constitute the biological upper limits of communicative and autonomous language uses. Within this context, genuine language disorders would be those that impair functioning of basic language proficiency. The rationale for positing a basic language proficiency construct does not appear compelling and the notion raises as many issues as it resolves: for example the role of socialization experiences in developing basic, autonomous and communicative proficiencies is unclear. If the development of basic proficiency is as much dependent on socialization as are autonomous and communicative proficiencies, then presumably genuine language disorders can be attributed, in part, to deficient socialization experiences. If both genuine disorders in basic language proficiency and difficulties in autonomous and communicative language proficiencies derive from deficiencies in socialization experiences then the distinctions between genuine language disorders and other forms of language difficulty (as well as between "basic" and other forms of proficiency) appears problematic.

Interdependence of L1 and L2 proficiencies

Genesee, Troike and Wald all raise the issue of L1–L2 relationships. This issue has been explicitly addressed in a recent study (Cummins et al., in press) where, on the basis of the results, a more general form of the interdependence hypothesis is proposed insofar as a distinction is made between *attribute-based* and *input-based* aspects of proficiency; the former show strong relationships across languages as a result of underlying cognitive or personality attributes of the individual, whereas the latter are more completely a function of exposure and input in L2. Thus, the point that Genesee raises about whether it is L1 academic mastery or age (or other factors) that predict L2 academic mastery is answered by pointing out that age and L1 academic mastery covary insofar as both are strongly related to the attribute of overall cognitive maturity.

Wald questions the extent to which the interdependence hypothesis is integrated into the context/cognition hypothesis. The connection between them is that the context/cognition framework goes some way towards elaborating the kinds of proficiency that transfer across languages in academic situations.

Troike's concern with the interdependence hypothesis relates to the perceived independence of CALP (or quadrant D) from the social context (an issue considered above) and also the nature of the CALP construct, namely whether it reduces to trivial test-taking skills and/or acculturation. Genesee, too, associates context-reduced proficiency with IQ tests and Wald suggests that "CALP skills are strictly test skills." These identifications misrepresent the construct of CALP or context-reduced proficiency insofar as they confuse the construct with one particular way of operationalizing it. CALP or quadrant D skills are developing from the child's first interactions and certainly long before s/he is exposed to any printed text. Hernandez-Chavez & Curtis (in press), for example, identify preschool "graphic sense" as one aspect of CALP and children's pattern of oral interaction with adults at age 2 predicts later acquisition of reading skills in school (see Wells, 1981). Similarly, CALP skills can be assessed by procedures such as miscue analysis (Bulcock & Beebe, 1981) and cloze measures as well as, or better than, by standardized tests (see Cummins & Swain, in press).

Cognitive demands and L1/L2 Acquisition

Wald suggests that I characterize L1 and L2 skills as showing the same progression in development and also that the cognitive demands of a child learning L1 are greater below the age of three than above it. These interpretations are certainly not what I intended to suggest. The fact that the framework is equally applicable to L1 and L2 acquisition does not imply that the processes and developmental sequence of L1 and L2 acquisition are identical. Also, the point about the early mastery of most aspects of phonology and syntax was not meant to imply that complete mastery occurred; rather that as mastery of subskills occurs the cognitive demands of the activity or task (i.e. subskills) decrease.

In summary, sociolinguistic considerations, which the authors in the present volume felt were neglected in the theoretical framework, can be incorporated more clearly by distinguishing between internal and external context. The sociopolitical underpinnings of the framework (and of bilingual education) have been considered in detail elsewhere (Cummins, 1982a) in ways which, I believe, would satisfy the concerns raised in the present volume. While there are many aspects of the relationship between language proficiency and academic progress which require both theoretical clarification and further research, the constructive dialogue across disciplinary boundaries initiated by the Language Proficiency Assessment Symposium will hopefully contribute substantially to resolving these issues.

References

Bulcock, J. W. and Beebe, M. J. 1981, Some common causes of literacy and numeracy. *Canadian Journal of Education*, 6, 19–44.
Cummins, J. 1979, Linguistic interdependence and the educational development of bilingual children. *Review of Educational Research*, 49(2), 222–51.
— 1980, The entry and exit fallacy in bilingual education. *NABE Journal*, 4(3), 25–60.
— 1981a, Age on arrival and immigrant second language learning in Canada: A reassessment. *Applied Linguistics*, 2(2), 132–49.
— 1981b, The role of primary language development in promoting educational success for language minority students. In California State Department of Education, *Schooling and language minority students: A theoretical framework*. Los Angeles: Evaluation, Dissemination and Assessment Center.
— 1982a, *Interdependence and bicultural ambivalence: Regarding the pedagogical rationale for bilingual education*. Rosslyn, VA.: National Clearinghouse for Bilingual Education.
— 1982b, *Language and literacy: Let's get back to the real basics!* Ontario Institute for Studies in Education, mimeo.
Cummins, J. & Swain, M. 1983, Analysis by rhetoric: Reading the text or the reader's own projections: A reply to Edelsky *et al.*, *Applied Linguistics*.
Cummins, J., Swain, M., Nakajima, K., Handscombe, J., Green, D. & Tran, C. In

press, *Linguistic interdependence among Japanese and Vietnamese immigrant students*. In C. Rivera (ed.), *Communicative Competence Approaches to Language Proficiency Assessment: Research and Application*. Clevedon, England: Multilingual Matters.

Hernandez-Chavez, E. & Curtis, J. in press, The graphic sense hypothesis: or You can't read firecrackers'. In C. Rivera (ed.), *Placement Procedures in Bilingual Education: Educational and Policy Issues*, Clevedon, England: Multilingual Matters.

McLaughlin, B. 1982, Theory in bilingual education. On misreading Cummins. University of California at Santa Cruz, mimeo.

Ogbu, J. 1978, *Minority education and caste*. New York: Academic Press.

Wells, G. 1981, *Learning through interaction: The study of language development*. New York: Cambridge University Press.

Index

Academic mastery 74
Accent 4, 60
Acculturation 38, 49
Age 24, 74
Age-appropriate proficiency 2, 9, 12
Analytic competence 29–31
Appropriateness conditions 36
Assessment of the Language Proficiency of Bilingual Persons project (ALPBP) x, xiii, xv
Assessment procedures 25
Australia ix, 49

Basic interpersonal communication skills (BICS) xix, xxi and CALP 4–5, 11–12, 19–21, 41, 45, 58–62
Basic Inventory of Natural Language (BINL) 8
Basic Language Competence Battery 7
Bernstein, B. 47
Bicultural ambivalence 72
Bilingual education 2
Bilingualism
 additive 45
 subtractive 45, 50
Bilingual Syntax Measure (BSM) 8
Black children 46, 50, 72

Canada 9, 45
Canadian French 4
Canale, M. xx, 13, 73
Caribbean ix
Centre for Research on Bilingualism xii
Chinese children 50
Chomsky, N. 42
Class domination 49
Cloze tests 60, 73
Cognitive-academic language proficiency (CALP) xix, xxi, 44, 46, 48–51, 74
 and BICS 4–5, 11–12, 19–21, 41, 47, 58–62
Cognitive advantages 2
Cognitive deficits 30, 37, 57
Cognitive demands 32, 34, 62, 65–6, 75
Cognitive development 35
Cognitive disadvantages 3
Cognitive involvement 13, 21, 31, 32
Coherence rules 35
Cohesion devices 35
Common underlying proficiency (CUP) 4
Communication
 context-dependent 31
 context-embedded 12–13, 22
 context-reduced 12–13
 written 63
Communicative activities 22
Communicative competence xiii, xv–xviii, 5, 11–13, 29, 42
Communicative proficiency xvi, 13, 35, 37
 interpersonal 31
Competence areas 34
Context-embedded situations 13, 16, 72
Context-embedding 62–3, 72
Context-reduced measures 16, 26
Contextual support 12, 21, 25, 31–3, 72
Contextual variables 35–6
Critical-age hypotheses 55
Cummins, J.
 Canale's critique 28–38
 Genesee's critique 20–7
 Spolsky's critique 41–3
 theoretical framework xvii, xix–xx, 2–19, 71–5

Troike's critique 45–51
Wald's critique 55–68
decontextualization 64
Department of Health, Education and Welfare (DHEW) x
Deutsch, K. 47
Developmental lag 24–6
Dialect 38
Discourse competence 34, 36
Dropping out 57

England 48
English as a Second Language (ESL) x, 9, 10, 15
English-only programs 8–9
Entry and Exit Procedures in Bilingual Education: Educational and Policy Issues xvii
Entry/exit criteria x, xi, xiii, xvi, xvii, 60, 67
 assessment of 2–3, 6, 15–17
 and CALP 20–1
 dilemma of 25–7
Exit tests 26

Face-to-face communicative skills 10, 12, 62–3, 72
Falmouth Conference on Testing, Teaching and Learning, 1978 x, xi
Filipino children 50
Finland 49
Fluency 4, 14, 58, 60–1, 67
French ix, 4, 45

Genesee, F. xx, 71, 74
German ix
g factor of intelligence (Spearman) 46
glp (Oller) 46, 51
Grammar 29, 35
Grammatical competence 11, 34–6
Grammatical forms 35–6, 38
Guest-workers ix
Guyana 48

Hispanic children 50, 56, 58–9, 72
Hymes, D. 42, 45

Iceberg metaphor 45
Integrative tests 7

Intellectual ability 6–7
Interactive communication 63–4
Inter America Research Associates xv
Interdependence hypothesis 3, 4, 14, 44–5, 49–50, 65
 and context-cognition hypothesis 67, 74
Interlocutor tolerance 42–3
Inversion 66
IQ tests 26, 49, 74
 verbal 10, 58–9
 performance 10

Kloss, H. ix
Knowledge of the world 47, 51–2

Labov, W. 57–8, 66
Language acquisition xii, 65–6
Language Assessment Scales (LAS) 8
Language deficit 7
Language disorders 28, 30, 34–5, 73–4
Language distinctions 56
Language functioning xii
Language maintenance ix
Language proficiency 20–5
 academic 31
 age-appropriate 2, 9
 analytic 29–31
 assessment 5–6
 attribute-based 74
 autonomous 28, 34–6
 basic 28, 34–6, 73
 cognitive 4, 31
 communicative 4, 28–9, 34–6
 context-reduced 19, 74
 input-based 74
 linguistic 29
 social context 32
Language Proficiency Assessment (LPA) Symposium, 1981 xv–xviii, 19, 75
Language shift ix
Language skills 6, 24
Language use
 academic 21–2
 analytic 31
 context-embedded 33
 context-free 29, 31
 context-reduced 33

formulaic 33
non-academic 21
social factors 21
spoken 33
written 33
Language tasks 33
Learning problems 51, 56
Lexical ability 5
Lexical knowledge 11
Linguistic competence 29, 42
Linguistic deficits 28, 34, 37
Linguistic mismatch 72
Listening comprehension 62
Literacy skills 3, 5, 57–64, 67–8, 73

Meaning
  literal 34–6
  social 35
Measurement of Communicative Proficiency: Models and Application xvi
Memory, verbal 22
Middle class 48–9, 51, 56
Miscommunications, cross-linguistic 58–9
Miscue analysis 74

National Clearinghouse for Bilingual Education (NCBE) xviii
National Institute of Education
  ALPBP project xv
  grants xviii
  Teaching and Learning Program xii
Navajo 49
Negotiation of meaning 32–3
Nonstandard language 48, 57–8

OBEMLA xviii
Oller, J. W. 46, 51, 57
Oral communication 65
Oral comprehension 61
Oral language proficiency 16
Oral syntax comprehension 5
Out-of-school contexts 17

Phoneme production 5
Phonology 14, 65–6, 68, 75
Placement of students 25, 51
Population shifts ix

Pragmatic aspects of language 5
Problem solving 23, 30, 33, 36
Pronunciation 11, 13–14, 32, 34, 42, 58, 60–1
Pygmalion effect 48, 50

Racial inferiority/superiority 30
Reading Is Fundamental (RIF) program 46
Reading skills 4, 14, 16, 46–8, 50–1, 63
Requests for Proposals (RFPs) xviii

School achievement 47–9
Self-expression 23
Semilingualism 50
Sentence formation 34, 36, 42
Shared knowledge 63, 72
Shared reality 63
Social factors xxi, 21, 23, 32, 42, 71–3
Social interaction skills 46
Socialization 36–8, 73–4
Social stigma 56
Socio-cultural factors (SCF) 47
Socio-economic status (SES) 19, 24, 47, 50, 56
Sociolinguistic competence 34, 36
Sociolinguistic conventions 22
Sociolinguistic Ethnographic Approach to Language Proficiency Assessment xvi
Sociolinguistic ethnography 59
Sociolinguistic style 47–8
Spanish ix, 4, 8, 56, 59, 61, 68
Spearman, C. 46
Species minimum 29, 30, 32
Speech acts 42
Speech situations, naturally-occurring 7
Spelling 34
Spolsky, B. xx
Spontaneous language 57
Strategic competence 35–6
Subskill mastery 13, 23, 75
Surface fluency xix, 3
Sweden 44, 49–50
Syntax 13–14, 42, 65–6, 75

Teacher training xii
Terminological innovation 41–3

Testing xi, 38, 43, 46, 57
  context-embedded 25
  cultural bias 64
  interpretation xx, 29, 37
  methodologies xvi
  procedures 2
  validation xv, 6, 29, 37
  variation 5
Test-taking skills 59–60
Text-processing skills 51
Theoretical framework xvii, xix, 11, 15, 28–38, 71–5
Threshold hypothesis 3, 44, 49, 55
Total immersion programs 24
Transfer 65
Troike, R. xxi, 71–2, 74

Truancy 56

Universals 35, 73

Validation xv, xvii, xx, 6, 29, 37
Value judgements 41
Verbal thinking 23
Vocabulary 36, 47, 60

Wald, B. xxi, 72, 74–5
Wells, G. 64
Wh- questions 66
Word formation 34
Word lists, memorizing 22
Writing 14
  creative 23